A LIFE SKILLS MANUAL

PERSONAL CARE

CLEO CARRUTHERS DipCOT

WINSLOW PRESS

Telford Road, Bicester, Oxon OX6 0TS Tel : Bicester (0869) 244644

Cleo Carruthers qualified as an occupational therapist from the Dorset House School of Occupational Therapy, Oxford, in 1973 and since then she has worked in many areas of psychiatry.

She has a special interest in activities which develop independent living skills, in particular personal care and vocational rehabilitation. She has practised these with a wide range of clients both in this country and the USA. She worked in Chicago for four years in a Day Clinic which helped psychiatric patients with long-term needs to become independent in the community. Until recently she was Head Occupational Therapist at St John's Hospital, Aylesbury.

First published in 1987 by
Winslow Press, Telford Road, Bicester, Oxon OX6 0TS.
Revised 1990

ISBN 0 86388 046 0

02·171/Printed in Great Britain by Hobbs the Printers, Southampton

CONTENTS

This manual is full of practical observations and suggestions as to how we can help various groups improve their physical self. One reads with interest, and a certain amount of self evaluation, as the pages unfold and the common sense is clearly displayed. We are able to focus more clearly and objectively on those ideas of which one is aware, but we have perhaps glossed over partly because we assume they are common knowledge.

As a fellow professional I believe one can, in the current climate, go overboard on technological facts, jargon and methods; by producing this manual, the author has brought us down to earth and reminded us there is much we can do for many care groups simply, cheaply and effectively.

She has also by her research enabled us to proceed where she has left off rather than, as is so often the case, leaving us with the feeling that this could work but how do I start . . . the answer is here. More please.

M R Green
District Occupational Therapist
Wycombe Health Authority

Like many of you, I am involved in caring for people who, for various reasons, neglect their general health and personal appearance. For these people to be integrated back into the community, these skills have to be taught.

General Health and Personal Appearance . . . this we take for granted. Those of us who are teaching these aspects to our clients know the hours spent working out individual programmes, trying to remember if we have missed out an important issue.

This book supplies many of the answers. It contains many of the strategies and methods required to teach these skills, to groups and individual patients. It provides the basis and guidelines for working out a detailed care programme by following the well laid-out plans of action, or developing them to fit your own needs and presents a comprehensive list of addresses of people to contact for further information. I heartily recommend this book to all those involved in teaching these very important aspects of our daily life.

John Kitchen RMN
Senior Nurse Manager
Rehabilitation Psychiatry
St Johns Hospital
Aylesbury

My thanks to Richard for his time, patience and encouragement.

A primary aim of any rehabilitation programme is to equip a client with the skills and knowledge necessary to function at a maximum level of independence. This book focuses on one particular aspect of independence: Personal Care.

My purpose in writing this book has been to produce a comprehensive working manual for professionals involved in organising a personal-care training programme. It has been designed to reduce some of the time-consuming preparation necessary in planning a group.

There are two main sections, Health, and Personal Appearance, subdivided into twelve chapters. Each topic commences with a clearly stated learning objective followed by the basic information that a client needs to acquire. Methods of imparting this information, entitled 'Strategies' are suggested. Topics have been designed so that those parts which are relevant to a specific group of individuals can be selected with ease.

Section III, the last section of the book, provides a list of organisations which can offer further valuable information to supplement the information in the book. The type of resource material available from each organisation is described in detail and information I feel would be particularly useful in a group has been recommended.

Group leaders will, no doubt, develop other 'strategies' which are not included here and I would be very interested to hear of them.

Cleo Carruthers

SECTION 1

HEALTH

OBJECTIVES:

● To increase knowledge of effects of diet on health.
● To promote changes in food consumption to reduce risks to health.

Food Groups

Although people have different requirements for the different nutrients in foods, a healthy diet is considered these days to be one which is well-balanced, low in sugar, fat and salt and high in fibre.

Eating some foods from each of these five groups daily ensures that all nutrients are obtained.

Group 1	Group 2	Group 3	Group 4	Group 5
Cereals Pasta Bread	Lean Meat Poultry Eggs Offal Fish	Fruit Vegetables	Dairy foods eg, Milk Yogurt Butter	Non-dairy fats and oils, eg Margarine Cooking oils

Nutrients in the Diet

These are the raw materials needed for body repair, protection and good health. They include vitamins, proteins, carbohydrates, minerals, fats and water.

Vitamins

There are thirteen known vitamins, the most well-known being vitamins A, B, C, D, E and K.

Functions of Vitamins

Vitamin A	
Primary Food Sources	**Functions**
Dark green leafy vegetables, ie, cabbage, sprouts, broccoli, spinach, carrots, apricots, tomatoes, liver, dairy foods, eggs.	Body growth. Keeping skin in good condition. Good vision in dim light.

Vitamin B (A group of 8 vitamins)	
Primary Food Sources	**Functions**
Milk, cheese, liver, kidneys, heart, vegetables, cereals.	Combined with iron, proper formation of red blood cells in bone marrow – therefore prevents some types of anaemia. Helps with functioning of nervous system. Breaks down carbohydrates and releases energy.

Vitamin C	
Primary Food Sources	**Functions**
Citrus fruits, tomatoes, green vegetables, particularly cabbage and sprouts, potatoes, blackcurrants.	Prevents scurvy. Repairs skin wounds. Ensures that body cells are working properly.

Vitamin D	
Primary Food Sources	**Functions**
Oily fish, ie, mackerel, herring, sardines. Egg yolks, butter, margarine. The body can manufacture Vitamin D from sunlight.	Healthy bones and teeth; prevents rickets in children.

Vitamin E	
Primary Food Sources	**Functions**
Sprouting grains, wheatgerm.	To date, the function of this vitamin is not clearly understood. Deficiency of Vitamin E does not show any negative effects in humans.

Vitamin K	
Primary Food Sources	**Functions**
Leafy green vegetables.	Helps with clotting of blood after injury.

Proteins

There are many different types of proteins. They maintain the body's processes, playing a major role in forming body tissues. They are a basic constituent of every body cell and form part of the structure of bones and teeth, brain, liver, muscle, blood and hair.

Some foods containing protein are:
- ▶ peas
- ▶ baked beans
- ▶ oats
- ▶ rice
- ▶ wheat
- ▶ lean meat
- ▶ cheeses of most kinds, especially cheddar
- ▶ peanuts
- ▶ fish

Carbohydrates

There are two types of carbohydrate – sugars and starches. They are important for providing energy and warmth. Starches such as bread, potatoes, rice and spaghetti also contain proteins, minerals and vitamins and should therefore be included in the diet. Sugary foods should however be eaten in moderation as they are not essential to the body's needs.

Minerals

Minerals are essential to keep the body healthy. They are present in a lot of foods, and have a number of functions. These are some of the most well known ones:

Calcium
This helps to build strong bones and teeth, is necessary for the clotting of blood and for the healthy functioning of nerves and muscles. Calcium can be found in cheese and milk. Deficiency causes brittle bones which fracture more easily than healthy bones.

Iron
This is an important constituent of the blood. Deficiency causes anaemia, the symptoms of which are tiredness and breathlessness. Women who have heavy monthly losses of blood, or are pregnant may require iron supplements to prevent iron deficiency anaemia. Iron is found in red meat, liver, kidney and heart. It is also found in dark leafy vegetables, eggs, cereals and bread but is not absorbed so well from these sources.

Fluoride
Essential for the development of normal teeth, fluoride helps prevent tooth decay. It is found naturally in some water supplies and is added by many water authorities in areas where the content is low. It can also be obtained from fluoride tablets. Fluoride toothpaste also helps protect teeth.

Iodine
Deficiency of this mineral contributes to enlargement of the thyroid gland, or goitre. Iodine is obtained from fortified table salt and this condition is now rare.

Fats

Fats provide energy, help make some hormones and form cell structure. However, many people eat too much fat for their bodies' needs. There may be a link between a fatty diet and heart disease. It has been found in many people suffering from heart disease that a fat-like substance called cholesterol has built up in the arteries, consequently making the passage of blood through them harder and thus the work of the heart more difficult. Most of us eat too much fat in our diet. In addition to the risk of heart disease too much fat, because it is high in calories, causes us to put on weight. To promote better health it may be advisable to reduce the amount of fat consumed. Although the causes of heart disease are not yet fully understood, individual fats are known to either increase or decrease, or have no effect on, blood cholesterol levels.

Saturated Fats (mostly solid animal and dairy fats)

Hard margarines
Suet
White cooking fats
Butter
Coconut and palm oil
Hard cheeses
Cream cheeses
Cream

} These increase cholesterol in the blood.

Polyunsaturated fats (mostly plant fats and usually oils)

Vegetable oils: corn
safflower seed
sunflower seed   } These reduce
soyabean   cholesterol
oily fish   in the blood.
certain types of margarine)

Monounsaturated fats

Olive oil
Fat from poultry } These have no effect.

Water

Water is essential for life. The adult body is composed of two thirds water. A person can only survive for about two or three days without water. It contains no calories; it carries nutrients around the body, cools the body with sweat, removes waste materials and has many other vital functions. Water is taken in with the food we eat but it is essential to drink plenty of liquid each day to ensure an adequate fluid intake.

A Healthy Eating Plan

Diet and bodily health are directly related. In recent years there has been a great deal of research on the effect of diet on health. Although some theories have yet to be proved conclusively, many factors seem to strongly suggest a connection between certain diseases and the kinds of food we eat.

Doctors suggest that people should pay more attention to what they eat and recommend the following guidelines:

Eat a variety of foods

Eating a balanced diet will ensure that the body will get all the different nutrients it needs to function efficiently.

Eat more fibre

Fibre, or 'roughage', is now thought to be an important part of the diet, having several different functions. Among other things it is thought to prevent bowel diseases such as diverticulitis and haemor-rhoids, to prevent constipation and to stimulate the digestive system. Many people do not have enough fibre in their diet.

Fibre is obtained only from plant-based foods. High fibre foods consist of nearly all fruits and vegetables, beans, peas, lentils, wholemeal bread, oats, barley, bran, breakfast cereals.

Eat less salt

People suffering from high blood pressure are at risk of developing heart disease. Excessive salt in the diet is thought to be one cause of high blood pressure. A lot of processed foods contain large amounts of salt even though they may not taste salty. Most people take in more salt than the body needs. Reducing salt intake not only lessens the risk of ill-health, but improves the taste of food. Salt-free food might taste rather bland at first but gradually the natural flavours of foods will come through and be more appealing. Alternatively there are salt substitutes on the market which can replace salt on the table. Another way is to use herbs, spices and other flavourings more imaginatively to make food tastier without resorting to salt.

Reduce consumption of high cholesterol foods

Besides saturated fats, other foods high in cholesterol may contribute to heart disease. These include butter, red meat, milk and eggs which should all be reduced. Vegetable oils should be used in cooking in place of animal fats.

Eat less sugar

Too much sugar can make you fat and promote tooth decay. It has little nutritional value and most people eat too much. Brown sugar is no better for you than white refined sugar – they have the same calorie content and both are bad for the teeth. Sugar is an ingredient of many foods – not always the ones you would expect – savoury sauces and baked beans for example – as well as cakes, biscuits, jams and drinks. Like salt, sugar can mask the natural taste of foods, so cutting down will not only be more healthy but food may taste better as well. There are sugar substitutes which can be used, not just the familiar saccharine but substitutes that actually look like sugar and do not leave an unpleasant aftertaste – but it is better on the whole to try to adjust to less sugar in the diet.

Do not overeat

If you eat more food than your body can burn then the extra energy is stored as fat. There are tables that show ideal weights for men and women of different ages and heights but these can only be a rough guide because everybody's metabolism is different. Two women of the same age and build for example may eat the same foods in the same amounts, but one's weight could increase while the other's remains steady. Nobody really knows why this is. However most people have some idea of how much their bodies need and when they are eating too much. Being overweight has many disadvantages; ill-fitting clothes or difficulty finding attractive clothes that fit, shortness of breath, high blood pressure and heart disease are just some of the problems. Here are some ways of cutting down on high calorie foods:

▶ Don't eat between meals. If this is difficult, at least eat sensibly – eat an apple or orange or piece of cheese or raw vegetables instead of crisps or peanuts.

▶ Reduce the amount of fat consumed:

grill food instead of frying it

eat lean meat/cut away fat from meat before eating

drain fatty foods

eat less oily foods, eg eat tuna in brine instead of tuna in oil

drink skimmed milk

use low fat spread instead of butter.

▶ Eat less sugary foods:

drink low calorie drinks

cut down sugar in tea and coffee

buy canned fruit packed in natural fruit juice rather than syrup, which has a high sugar content

eat breakfast cereals without adding sugar

cut down on sweets, cakes and jams.

▶ Cut down size of helpings at meals – or decrease amount of high calorie food (eg pork) and increase amount of low calorie food (eg cabbage, carrots).

▶ Make sure you have three meals daily. Some people do not eat breakfast; this is not a good habit as it can cause you to feel more hungry later in the day than you would otherwise.

▶ Fibre is filling. Besides its other important functions an added bonus is that fibre-rich foods are satisfying. Fill up on these rather than sugary and fatty foods.

Slimming Diets

Despite the numerous types of reducing diet most doctors still agree that there is only one effective way to lose weight – to take in less calories than your body needs. This can be done by selectively reducing the intake of food or by increasing physical activity and burning up more energy. Doing both together is even more effective. Research has shown that many people who successfully lose weight by dieting put it all back on again within a year or two and in some cases even gain weight. This is because most people return to their old eating pattern – a pattern which made them overweight in the first place. So if a diet is going to have any lasting benefits, it should be a healthy one with a variety of foods, high in fibre and with plenty of fresh fruit and vegetables, and should be viewed as the start of a more considered, nutritious and healthy way of eating for the future.

'Crank' diets are best avoided. A doctor can advise on a suitable diet and it is wise to seek medical supervision when embarking on one.

Convenience Foods

Packaged food is easy and quick to prepare; there is no wastage and not much washing up and it can be just as nutritious as fresh food – even more so if you have a tendency to over-cook vegetables and fruit, which reduces its nutritional value. There is also now a wide choice of convenience foods available. However, pre-packed food is usually more expensive than preparing a dish from raw ingredients. Also many convenience foods contain colourings, flavourings and preservatives. It is probably best to eat a combination of both convenience foods and fresh foods if there is a tendency to depend on convenience foods as this will help to avoid any nutritional deficiencies.

The Vegetarian Diet

These days people are tending to eat less red meat or even to cut it out of their diet altogether for health reasons. Other people may not eat meat for religious reasons. Many people misunderstand vegetarianism, and think it means eating beans and rice and not much else, but in fact vegetarian food can be varied, attractive and tasty. Vegetarian cookery books offer a wealth of ideas.

There are two types of vegetarian – the lacto-vegetarian and the vegan. Lacto-vegetarians avoid red meat but eat dairy products and sometimes eggs. They should not have any nutritional problems. The vegan diet is more restrictive; vegans eat vegetable foods only and exclude all animal products – including gelatine, milk, cheese, meat, eggs and fish. They need to be sure of getting enough iron in their diet. Vitamin B12 which is found mainly in animal foods can also be deficient.

Food Supply

Build up a supply of pictures (mounted on card for a longer life), empty cans and packets of a wide variety of common foods. These can be used again and again in many different ways. Some suggested uses are:

▶ To gain a realistic knowledge of food prices.

▶ To increase awareness of nutrition and the meaning of a balanced diet; planning menus.

▶ To gain a better understanding of ingredients listed on packets, particularly for those on restricted diets. For example 'salt' may often be shown as 'sodium'.

▶ To learn how to follow recommended cooking instructions.

Relaxation and Fantasy

This is a useful introduction to aspects of health care. Particular aspects such as diet or fitness can be emphasised depending on the particular needs of the group.

Part I

Group members are asked to imagine that each of them has won a competition to spend a week on a health farm. They should lie down and relax in a comfortable position and they will be told all about it.

The room should be comfortable, warm and darkened during the relaxation session. If the members are all women, they can be invited, before this part of the session, to apply face packs and eye pads (cotton wool dampened in water or cucumber slices), and lie with legs raised slightly on a cushion or low chair. This can aid relaxation, strengthen the fantasy and improve the skin all at the same time.

The leader of the group should describe, in a soft voice, the health farm. The countryside could be vividly described, the luxurious furnishings, swimming in a warm, scented pool, etc.

Some of the services offered by the establishment are described in detail as if each person is acutally receiving it at that moment. It should be described in the most appealing or relaxing way, eg – face massage – 'you are lying back upon great, soft cushions in a big comfortable armchair with eyes closed. Someone is standing behind the chair massaging your temples'.

At the conclusion of the fantasy, the members are told that they feel completely revitalised, healthy, full of energy and they are ready to return home and continue leading a more healthy and enjoyable lifestyle.

The relaxation session ends and if members have worn face packs, they can now wash them off.

Part II

The exercise continues by displaying a list on a blackboard or flipchart of many of the improvements to health offered by the health farm including those already described. The list could look something like this:

1 Improved muscle tone
2 Improved level of fitness
3 A healthier diet
4 Weight loss
5 More energy
6 Stop smoking
7 Other

Each member is asked to imagine that when they arrived at the health farm they were presented with this list and asked to put a tick beside all the things they wanted to improve. Each person is then asked to list the things they would have chosen in order of priority on a piece of paper. Each member then talks about their list – what they have chosen and why.

Dear Dr Jones

Before the group, cut out letters published in magazines relating to diet and health issues. Each group member is given a letter to read out to the group. The group then discusses the letter and what would be the appropriate advice to give the letter-writer. The letters selected should, of course, be relevant to the group.

Fat Harry and Slim Suzy

(Thanks to Rachel Scott, DipCOT, for this exercise)

Take two large pieces of paper; on one, draw the outline of Fat Harry and on the other, Slim Suzy. They should look something like this:

Fat Harry   Slim Suzy

The group then cuts out pictures of food from magazines. Foods which are very fattening, particularly those high in sugar, fat or starch should be stuck, at random, on Fat Harry's stomach. Those which are low in calories are stuck inside the outline of Slim Suzy. When both collages are complete, a discussion can ensue about diet and weight and any relevant points which have arisen should be added, in bold writing, to one or other collage. A statement such as 'Fried potatoes are more fattening than boiled potatoes', can be written by Harry, for example.

Diet and Health Quiz

1) Which of the following is the average Briton not eating enough of?
A. Protein
B. Vitamins
C. Roughage

Answer: **C** – *Prevents constipation and has other health benefits.*

2) Which of the following is the average Briton eating too much of?
A. Fatty food
B. Frozen vegetables
C. Breakfast cereals

Answer: **A** – *High in calories and may be linked to heart disease.*

3) Which of the following foods is the most fattening?
A. Wholemeal bread
B. Jacket potatoes
C. Salted peanuts

Answer: **C** – *Nearly three times as many calories as wholemeal bread.*

4) Apart from looking and feeling better, what is the main benefit of staying slim?
A. You can eat bigger meals
B. You can think faster
C. It helps your heart and arteries stay younger longer

Answer: **C** – *Helps avoid heart attacks and high blood pressure.*

5) Which of these fats is thought to increase the amount of cholesterol in the blood?
A. Olive oil
B. Corn oil
C. Butter

Answer: **C** – *Butter is a saturated fat – which is thought to increase cholesterol levels in the body.*

6) A balanced diet means:
A. Eating more vegetables and fruit
B. Eating less meat and more fish
C. Eating a variety of foods daily from the five food groups

Answer: **C** – *Eating a variety of foods will provide all the nutrients needed by the body.*

7) Reducing our intake of foods high in cholesterol besides saturated fats will help decrease the chance of heart disease. Which of the following foods is high in cholesterol?
A. Eggs
B. Fish
C. Spinach

Answer: **A** – *Doctors recommend that we should eat fewer eggs. No more than two a week is considered advisable.*

8) Which of the following foods provides fibre?
A. Bacon
B. Potatoes
C. Yogurt

Answer: **B** – *Only plant-based foods contain fibre.*

9) Which of the following, when used excessively, is thought to be a cause of high blood pressure?
A. Sugar
B. Pepper
C. Salt

Answer: **C** – *Most people's intake of salt is far in excess of the body's needs.*

10) Which of these cheeses contains most fat?
A. Cheddar
B. Curd Cheese
C. Cottage Cheese

Answer: **A** – *Cheddar has 33.5% fat, curd cheese about 11% and cottage cheese 4%.*

(Parts of this quiz are reproduced with the kind permission of the Health Education Authority.)

2: FITNESS

What is fitness?

Physical fitness consists of several factors:

Stamina

The heart is the most important muscle of the body. Like any muscle it benefits from being exercised. Exercising the heart makes it stronger. Stamina involves the arteries and the lungs which also benefit, and all the muscle groups of the body.

Flexibility

Flexibility or suppleness depends on movement. The less mobile we are, the more stiff we are likely to become as we grow older.

Strength

We need strength for activities of daily living such as lifting heavy loads, or doing heavy physical work such as digging. Exercises which increase strength help to tone up muscles.

Weight

Keeping your body active can also help you control your weight. The body's metabolism changes within a regular fitness programme and burns more calories.

What are the benefits of regular exercise?
► Exercise improves the staying power of your heart and circulation and may protect against coronary heart disease.
► It keeps your neck, back and joints supple and your posture correct.
► It tightens flabby muscles and gives you strength.

► It helps you stay slim.
► It helps combat stress.
► It can be great fun.
► It helps you feel good, in mind as well as body.

Precautions

Before undertaking any fitness programme a doctor should be consulted if there are any doubts about one's general health. If one or more of the following questions can be answered with a "yes" a doctor should be seen.
► Have you ever suffered from any form of heart trouble?
► Do you frequently have pains in the heart or chest?
► Do you often feel faint or have spells of severe dizziness?
► Has your doctor ever said your blood pressure was too high?
► Has your doctor ever told you that you have a bone or joint problem such as arthritis, that may be aggravated by exercise?
► Is there a good physical reason not mentioned here why you should not undertake a programme of regular exercise?
► Are you over 65 years of age and not accustomed to exercise?

(Reproduced from the Fit for Life Casebook *published by the Scottish Sports Council/Scottish Health Education Group. Now out of print.)*

Getting Fit

Consider these factors when developing a fitness programme:
Choose an enjoyable activity
Even a daily exercise routine on the living-room floor can be made more enjoyable by varying the exercises from time to time, using an exercise tape, following the exercises on a TV programme etc.
Make practical use of daily activities
Don't use the escalator, use the stairs. Walk instead of taking the bus — or get off one stop before your destination. Walk briskly. Cycle to work instead of driving the car. Walk the dog regularly. Slowly stretch all the parts of your body as you wake up in the morning.

Decide whether you would prefer exercising indoors or outdoors

There are plenty of fitness activities to choose from and if it matters to you whether you get your exercise indoors or out you shouldn't have too much trouble finding the right one.

Start slowly

It's easy to overdo it at the beginning if you are out of condition. Build up slowly, and within your capability. If you have aching muscles at the beginning, warm baths will help. If the exercise is kept up, the aches and pains will soon disappear. Stretching exercises will also help limber up the body before doing any vigorous activity and help avoid pulled muscles or other strains.

Exercise regularly

If regular exercise becomes a natural part of daily life it will not only build up and sustain your fitness level but will also make it less likely that you'll give up. Exercise needs to be taken at least three times a week for about twenty minutes each time for there to be a positive benefit. Benefits should begin to show in about six to seven weeks.

Wear the right clothing

This is particularly important where footwear is concerned. For example a pair of well-fitting running shoes is essential for jogging. Comfort is also important. Comfortable clothes should allow you to move properly. The type of material may also be important particularly if the exercise is vigorous.

Plan a seasonal fitness programme

For example, if you regularly take part in a summer sport you will have to plan alternative exercise for the off-season so that you can keep fit all year round.

Do not exercise right after eating a meal

It is uncomfortable and can be dangerous. Wait one to two hours for food to be digested.

Exercise Activities

The table below shows the ratings of different activities with regard to stamina, suppleness and strength. This is followed by an additional list of further suggestions for exercise activities:

(Table reproduced with the permission of the Health Education Authority.)

	Stamina	Suppleness	Strength
Badminton	●●	●●●	●●
Canoeing	●●●	●●	●●●
Climbing stairs	●●●	●	●●
Cricket	●	●●	●
Cycling (hard)	●●●●	●●	●●●
Dancing (ballroom)	●	●●●	●
Dancing (disco)	●●●	●●●●	●
Digging (garden)	●●●	●●	●●●●
Football	●●●	●●●	●●●
Golf	●	●●	●
Gymnastics	●●	●●●●	●●●
Hill walking	●●●	●	●●
Housework (moderate)	●	●●	●
Jogging	●●●●	●●	●●
Judo	●●	●●●●	●●
Mowing lawn by hand	●●	●	●●●
Rowing	●●●●	●●	●●●●
Sailing	●	●●	●●
Squash	●●●	●●●	●●
Swimming (hard)	●●●●	●●●●	●●●●
Tennis	●●	●●●	●●
Walking (briskly)	●●	●	●
Weightlifting	●	●	●●●●
Yoga	●	●●●●	●

● No real effect ●● Beneficial effect ●●● Very good effect ●●●● Excellent effect

Further suggestions for exercise activities:

Skiing; Skipping; Basketball; Hockey; Horseriding; Rugby; Orienteering; Table tennis; Volleyball; Keep fit classes; Aerobics.

The Facts About Smoking

Smoking is:

► Expensive.
► Unpleasant to smell.
► A common cause of fires.
► Strongly associated with ill-health, in particular:
  lung cancer (nearly all lung cancer is caused by smoking)
  bronchitis and emphysema
  coronary heart disease
  miscarriages, low birth weight and abnormalities in the new born child.

In addition it diminishes your senses of smell and taste, the smoke can be offensive to others and anti-social and nicotine stains fingers and teeth.

Smoking clinics

These are available on the NHS and privately. A GP will advise. They are self-help groups where several smokers get together and help each other stop smoking by discussing the problems and by developing individual programmes. Motivation to stop is important.

Minor Illnesses and Common Complaints

The Common Cold

As yet there is no cure for the common cold and the great claims made for Vitamin C – that in large doses it can prevent colds – have not been proved. The symptoms, however, can be relieved by various commercial preparations. A cold in an otherwise healthy adult would not normally require medical attention. Complications can arise, however, such as laryngitis, bronchitis or an ear infection, in which case a doctor should be consulted.

Influenza

Flu is caused by a virus. Vaccination is only partially effective because it is impossible to predict which of the many types of virus will be responsible for the outbreak in any one year. Common symptoms are a rapid rise in temperature, aching, shivering, possibly a sore throat and headache. Flu usually lasts two to three days and unless the symptoms continue unabated medical attention is not normally necessary. Commercial remedies will help alleviate some of the discomfort and bedrest will also help.

Gastric Flu

Similar to influenza but with vomiting or diarrhoea or both. This is very uncomfortable but usually symptoms disappear after two or three days. The best treatment is to avoid eating any food for the first day or two but to drink plenty of juice with a little salt added to prevent dehydration. Bedrest is advisable and extreme tiredness is common. It is advisable to see the doctor to ensure that there is not a more serious case of food poisoning.

Headaches

These take different forms, some more serious than others. For the occasional headache, medication such as paracetamol, in the prescribed dose, should be sufficient. Migraine, the cause of which is still unknown, is a severe pain often preceded by disturbances in speech, sight or hearing, a feeling of nausea or actual vomiting. Medical treatment should be sought. Sinusitis often causes a headache, usually situated in the region of the forehead and is associated with blocked nasal passages. Effective medication can be obtained from a chemist.

Throat infections

Characterized by a sore throat, this often heralds a cold or influenza without any further complications. It will usually get better within a few days. Lozenges and honey and lemon drinks will soothe some of the discomfort. If the infection persists or if lumps appear in the neck, indicating that the infection has spread to the lymph glands, medical advice should be sought.

First Aid in Self-Care

First aid kits can be bought complete or can be made up by purchasing individual items and storing them in a plastic box or biscuit tin with a well-fitting lid. It should not be stored in the bathroom because moisture could affect the contents. If there are children in the house it should be kept out of reach or locked away. Any medicines should be kept in child-proof containers and should be clearly labelled. Medications which have not been used up should be discarded by throwing them away or returning them to the chemist.

Suggested list of contents for a first-aid kit:

Rolled gauze bandages in assorted sizes
Scissors *(with rounded ends preferably)*
Aspirin or paracetamol tablets *(for pain relief)*
A roll of adhesive tape *(to attach dressings and bandages)*
Tweezers *(pointed type – to remove insect stings, glass from cuts, etc)*
Calamine lotion *(for sunburn or reddened skin)*
Crêpe bandages *(to provide support, for example in a sprain)*
Safety pins *(for securing bandages)*   Cotton wool
Assorted plasters   Thermometer
Eye pads   Antiseptic wipes
Triangular bandage   First aid book

Treatment of Minor Accidents

Minor burns and scalds

For a major burn or scald, medical help must be sought immediately. A small injury should be cooled immediately after the accident by running cold water over it or immersing the burn in cold water for ten minutes. Cover with a dry, non-stick, sterile dressing if necessary.

Cuts and grazes

Remove anything sticking to the wound such as gravel. Next, wash the wound, if it is small, by holding it under cold running water. Alternatively clean it with cotton wool or gauze moistened with water or diluted disinfectant. Clean away from the wound so that more dirt does not enter. Dry and apply an adhesive dressing.

Planning a Fitness Programme

This exercise uses some of the subheadings to be found on page 10 under *Getting Fit* and helps the individual who is unaccustomed to exercise plan a programme suited to their interests and needs. A spider diagram is used – the method being demonstrated first by the group leader on a blackboard or large sheet of paper. In the centre of the page the person writes their name. Subheadings are then written around the name and the individual writes beneath what applies to him or her. An example is given below:

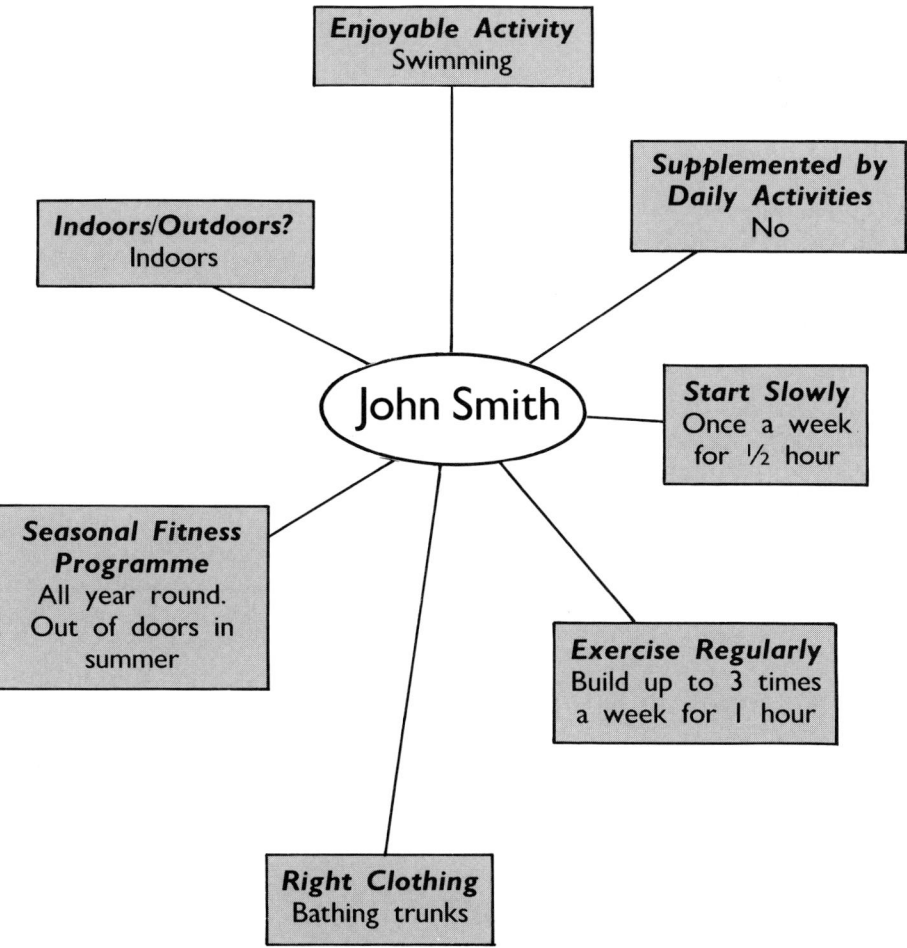

Evaluating Activities

Try out as a group as many different types of exercise as possible within the scope of facilities and equipment available. Some possible activities might be floor exercises, badminton, jogging, volleyball, swimming at the local pool, walking, etc.

Encourage members of the group to suggest activities they might be interested in trying. Perhaps some of them have always wanted to try a particular activity but have never got around to it. Or they may have had a favourite activity which has lapsed that they may like to return to.

After each activity promote a discussion about how individuals felt about the activity, eg did they enjoy it; is it something that they would like to continue; would cost very much to do, etc.

If there is a local sports or leisure centre, a visit can be arranged as a group to find out what is available, charges, opening times, etc. Libraries are also a good source of information on classes in the area.

A Stop Smoking Plan

Assistance in giving up smoking would be most effective if all members in the group were smokers and so could provide each other with support, understanding and a common identity. The chances of giving up will be increased if members volunteer for this group and are motivated to stop smoking.

Each member is provided with a small pocket-size notebook and instructed that all the information which follows should be written in it. They should carry the notebook with them at all times and if they feel a strong craving to smoke, should take it out and read the notes that it contains. Ask each person to write their name on the book.

Discuss as a group: Why each person wants to give up smoking. These facts may help:

▶ 95,000 people in this country die before their time because of smoking *every year*.

▶ Out of 1000 young people who smoke, six will be killed by traffic accidents and 250 will be killed by smoking.

▶ The average person killed by smoking loses ten to fifteen years of life.

▶ Smokers are much more likely to have a heart attack or be crippled by bronchitis.

▶ The risk of smokers contracting lung cancer is up to 25 times more than non-smokers.

▶ The chances are that every cigarette you smoke will shorten your life by 5½ minutes.

Members of the group should write into their notebooks all the reasons for giving up arising out of the discussion, under the title 'Why I should give up smoking'.

Discuss as a group: What will each person gain by giving up smoking? These facts may help:

▶ Giving up brings immediate results.

▶ Risk of heart attack, bronchitis and lung cancer will decrease.

▶ Shortage of breath improves.

▶ Smokers cough will improve.

▶ No more yellow fingers and teeth.

▶ Clean-smelling hair, breath and clothes.

▶ An unborn baby will stand a better chance of being born healthy.

▶ One's children will be less likely to start smoking.

▶ Money can be spent on other things – work out how much you have spent on cigarettes during the past year.

Members are asked to write into their notebooks in the first person points arising from the discussion.

Discuss as a group: Ways of giving up smoking.

Some members may already have decided on a particular method they would like to try. Otherwise – here are four different methods which should be described and then discussed. Each group member is asked to choose one of them.

Programme I
Switch off slowly, but steadily. Decide that each day you are going to have your first cigarette one hour later than you did the day before. What you will be doing is cutting out your first cigarette of the day, then the second, and the third, and so on until you stop altogether.

Programme II
Set a date. Write it in the notebook. Make up your mind you want to stop on a certain day and decide on that day two or three weeks in advance. During that time reduce your smoking bit by bit, then stop for good on the chosen day.

Programme III

Work out the times when you are most likely to want to smoke a cigarette; after a meal, for instance, or with a cup of coffee, or when you are reading or watching TV. Be strong and cut them out. You will be left smoking the cigarettes that you get the least pleasure from. It shouldn't be too difficult to cut these out too.

Programme IV

Make a rule. Make a rule not to smoke while doing certain things – driving, working or when out of doors, for instance. Bring two or three activities together and don't smoke during this time.

Helpful Tips

▶ Tell people you are giving up smoking and tell them when.

▶ Use no-smoking compartments on buses and trains.

▶ Avoid friends who still smoke, for a few days at least.

▶ Put aside the money you save each day. Plan to spend it on some kind of reward for yourself.

▶ Keep busy.

▶ Keep a supply of things to nibble on – dried fruit, nuts, sugarless chewing gum.

▶ Take each day as it comes.

The group members should now monitor each other's progress and support each other's efforts to give up. Each person should, at the start of their chosen programme, draw up a calendar in the notebook and record their progress daily. This can be shown to the rest of the group and discussed. Here is an example of a calendar which has been filled in over a two week period:

Mon	0
Tues	I (After dinner)
Wed	0
Thurs	2 (Teabreak, lunch)
Fri	I (2-hour train journey)
Sat	0
Sun	0

Mon	0
Tues	I (After dinner)
Wed	0
Thurs	0
Fri	I (Lunch)
Sat	I
Sun	0

Looking at this record, it might be concluded that this person finds not smoking at meal times particularly difficult. The long train journey also suggests that inactivity or boredom also promote a craving for cigarettes. Part of the function of the group would be to suggest ways of overcoming these hard times.

(Parts of this programme are reproduced by kind permission of the Scottish Sports Council, Scottish Health Education Group and Health Education Authority.)

First Aid Box

Display the contents of a first aid box and ask members how each item would be used. Discuss accidents in the home. Ask members to demonstrate how to treat minor burns or scalds, cuts and grazes, etc.

Emergency

Ask members to role-play what to do in an emergency. Describe a particular situation. How would they summon help?

Emergency Information List

Provide each member of the group with a sheet of paper which has printed on the left-hand side the following:

FIRE / POLICE / AMBULANCE: Dial 999

DOCTOR: TELEPHONE:

ADDRESS: SURGERY HOURS:

NEAREST TAXI SERVICE-TELEPHONE:

DENTIST: TELEPHONE: ADDRESS: SURGERY HOURS:

PEOPLE TO CONTACT IN AN EMERGENCY:

NAME: TELEPHONE: (Home) (Work)

ADDRESS:

NAME:

TELEPHONE: (Home) (Work)

ADDRESS:

Ask members to fill in the right-hand side with the appropriate information. The sheet is theirs to keep and refer to in the event of an emergency. It should be kept in an accessible place and updated when necessary. Other useful information can be added to it if desired.

Fitness and Health Quiz

1) Apart from feeling fitter and healthier what is the main benefit of regular exercise?

A. It tones up your complexion
B. It gives you a healthy appetite
C. It helps your heart and arteries stay younger longer.

Answer: C – Helps avoid heart attacks and strokes.

2) Regular exercise can build up your strength, develop your stamina and keep you supple. Which is most important for protecting your heart?

A. Strength
B. Stamina
C. Suppleness

Answer: B – Improves the efficiency of your circulation.

3) Which is the best indication that the exercise you are doing is helping to build up stamina?

A. It makes you sweat a lot
B. It makes you slightly breathless
C. It makes your muscles ache a little.

Answer: B – Because your heart and lungs are being well exercised.

4) Here are three forms of exercise. Assuming you practise regularly, which one is best for developing stamina?

A. Vigorous swimming
B. Yoga
C. Weight-lifting

Answer: A – Dynamic exercise using large muscles.

5) It's been at least five or six years since you had any form of regular exercise. You are overweight and out of condition and have decided to start a daily exercise routine. Which of these three would be the best choice of exercise to begin with?

A. A daily two-mile jog
B. Squash
C. Half an hour of brisk walking daily

Answer: C – Building up gradually to more vigorous exercise as stamina improves.

6) To gain positive benefits from exercise what is the minimum recommended number of sessions that should be taken each week?

A. A twenty-minute session three times a week
B. A one-hour session three times a week
C. A tcn-minute session four times a week

Answer: A – Will give the most benefit.

7) Smoking is hazardous to your health. It is a major cause of:

A. Coughs and colds
B. Lung cancer and heart disease
C. Migraine

Answer: B – Most lung cancer is caused by smoking.

8) Before taking part in any active activity it's a good idea to:

A. Have a rest
B. Have a drink in case you get thirsty
C. Warm up first

Answer: C – To keep joints flexible, and avoid pulling muscles and tendons.

(Parts of this quiz are reproduced with kind permission of the Health Education Authority.)

OBJECTIVES:

● To foster an understanding of women's natural body functions and their effects on health.
● To learn effective methods of coping with or preventing disorders in women.

The Menstrual Cycle

The menstrual cycle lasts on average 28 days but there are no hard and fast rules and for many women their cycle may be longer or shorter. Irregular cycles are quite common and the length may also vary from one month to the next. In addition some women experience heavy bleeding while others have light bleeding. Light bleeding is often a characteristic of women on the pill. It is also quite common for a period to be heavy at the beginning and lighter as the days go on. Four to six days is the average time that a period lasts but it can last anything from two to eight days.

All women are born with all the eggs they will ever have, in their ovaries. Each one of these eggs will be released from an ovary and travel down towards the uterus. This is called ovulation; this is the time of the month when a woman is most fertile. If the egg is fertilized with sperm from the male it will then attach itself to the lining of the uterus which has thickened in readiness to receive a fertilized egg. A baby will then start to grow. If, however, the egg has not been fertilized, the uterus will shed its lining which is made up of blood and tissue and this, along with the egg will be discharged from the body. This is a period. This whole cycle is repeated monthly.

Women's Ailments

Pre-menstrual Syndrome (pre-menstrual tension, or PMT)

Pre-menstrual syndrome is a collection of symptoms and bodily changes that occur, usually on a regular basis, anything from a few days to two weeks before a woman's period, and cease, or reduce significantly, with its arrival. Over a hundred different symptoms have been described in the pre-menstrual syndrome.

However by far the commonest are such complaints as nervous tension, mood swings, irritability, weight gain, breast tenderness and headache to name but a few. It is thought that approximately 30-40% of women of child-bearing age may suffer significant pre-menstrual symptoms.

(Reproduced with permission from the Pre-menstrual Tension Advisory Service.)

Some other symptoms reported by women suffering from PMT are: water retention, insomnia, muscle stiffness, fatigue, backache, cramps, dizziness, nausea, poor concentration, hot flushes and fainting.

Cause

PMT is thought to be caused by an imbalance in the sex hormones which control the reproductive cycle.

How to cope with PMT

▶ See your GP. A GP may prescribe short-term hormone supplements. Vitamin B6 can also help some women. It is known that a deficiency of B6 can contribute to PMT. The pill can relieve the symptoms in some women, but can make them worse for others.

▶ Visit a 'well-woman' clinic.

▶ Try to set aside some time to relax every day.

Period Pain

Period pain is a result of strong contractions of the muscular uterus wall as it sheds its lining. The pain may be accompanied by tiredness, headaches and in more severe cases, nausea or vomiting.

Coping with period pain

▶ Some women find that exercise helps — whether a sport, or some keep-fit exercises.

► Some commercial preparations can be effective in relieving period pain.

► Painful periods often disappear when a woman starts taking the Pill.

► See your GP – who may prescribe drug treatment or refer you to a gynaecologist who may suggest a D & C (dilation and curettage). Under a general anaesthetic, the lining of the womb is scraped. This often affords relief but why it does is not well understood.

If severe period pains suddenly occur for the first time after several years of pain-free menstruation then it is important to consult a doctor.

Vaginal Infections

These are common and there are different types. It is important to see the doctor to determine the type of infection and get appropriate treatment. Discomfort due to irritation and a discharge are the usual symptoms. Infection can be due to a fungus or a parasite.

Preventing Vaginal Infections

► Wash genital area every day.

► Wear clean underwear every day.

► Avoid deodorants and vaginal sprays.

► When using toilet paper wipe from front to back.

► Urinate after sexual contact.

► Sometimes synthetic fibres which retain heat and moisture are best avoided eg nylon underwear, tights and tight trousers.

► Using a condom during sexual intercourse reduces the chances of transmitting infections.

Cystitis

This is a urinary infection and is a common complaint. The bladder becomes inflamed and often the urethra, the tube through which urine is passed out of the body, becomes inflamed too. Cystitis is much more common in women than men and symptoms vary. It is common to feel discomfort – a burning sensation when passing urine;

dark coloured urine; an ache in the lower abdomen; a frequent "bursting" feeling of wanting to pass water but actually only passing an insignificant amount. A doctor should be consulted but it helps to relieve the symptoms if fruit drinks, water, milk or weak tea are drunk in copious amounts at the first sign of an attack.

The Menopause

Men are fertile until the end of their lives. Women, on the other hand, undergo a change at mid-life and become incapable of bearing any more children. This change is known as the menopause. Between the ages of about 42 and 52 periods become irregular and eventually stop. They may become heavier or lighter. Changes in hormone levels may affect a woman's moods. Hot flushes may occur and some women find that they tend to put on weight. This is a slow process and it may appear that the menopause has ended when suddenly a period comes again. This is a not unusual occurrence and it is important to continue practising birth control until advised by a doctor that it is safe to abandon it as the woman is no longer fertile. A doctor can also help relieve some symptoms of the menopause.

Preventive Care

The Smear Test

The Cytotest (smear test) is a simple test that prevents cancer by spotting changes at the neck of the womb (cervix) before cancer develops. It is important for all women especially those over thirty-five. The test may also show up other small problems which can easily be treated. It only takes a few minutes and simply involves taking a smear of fluid from the cervix. This is then examined in a laboratory. The test should be done every five years up to sixty five and is widely available under the NHS. It can detect pre-cancerous cells in the neck of the womb anything up to 15 or 20 years before they become invasive and they can be treated easily and successfully.

Breast Self-examination

There is at present no comparable screening test available which will detect breast cancer. Breast cancer can be cured if it is treated soon enough; and most of the women who are cured are women who have discovered the cancer themselves, so it is very important to check your breasts regularly yourself. The method is outlined below:

WHAT TO CHECK FOR

Check your breasts every month. Just after a period is a good time or if you don't have them, the same day each month.

When you check, relax and don't hurry. Remember you are looking for a change, something unusual *for you*. So the first time, note:

▶ The normal size and shape of your breasts.

▶ The normal position of your nipples.

▶ The normal feel of your breasts (they may well be naturally lumpy, especially before a period).

Then each time you check, ask yourself these five questions:

Size and shape: Is there any change?

Nipples: Does either turn in on itself, or point up and outwards unusually? Are they bleeding or weeping?

Breast surface: Any unusual swelling or dimple? Do the veins stand out more than usual?

Skin: Is it puckered? Is there a rash or any odd colour?

Feel: Is there any lump or thickening?

If the answer to any of these questions is yes, see your doctor at once. Most breast trouble is *not* due to cancer, but can be troublesome if not treated promptly. Even if it is cancer, it can be cured if treated soon enough – sometimes even without an operation.

HOW TO LOOK

Undressed to the waist, sit in front of a mirror in a good light.

Look: Hands at your sides or on your hips, look carefully at your breasts. Turn from side to side. Look underneath too.

Lift: Hands on your head, look for anything unusual, especially around the nipple.

Stretch: Arms stretched above your head, look again, particularly around the nipple.

Press: Hands on hips, press inwards until your chest muscles tighten. Look again, especially for any dimpling of the skin.

HOW TO FEEL

Lie on a flat surface, head on a pillow, shoulder slightly raised by a folded towel.

▶ Left shoulder raised, feel the left breast with the right hand. Use the flat of the fingers, keeping them together.

▶ Press the breast gently but firmly in towards the body. Work in a spiral, circling out from the nipple. Feel every part.

▶ Left arm above your head, elbow bent, repeat the spiral carefully. Feel the outer part of the breast especially. Finish by feeling the tail of the breast towards the armpit.

Repeat all four stages on the other breast. Be thorough. Don't rush.

(Reproduced courtesy of the Women's National Cancer Control Campaign.)

DISCUSSION TOPICS:

● Do any of the group members experience any discomfort related to their monthly cycle or to the menopause?
● What is the nature of the discomfort?
● Have they discovered any particularly effective ways of alleviating the discomfort?

Preventative Care

A breast check should be done in private and needs time and practice for it to be performed with confidence. Films, posters or leaflets would be particularly helpful as aids.

Group members can each be provided with a sheet of paper clearly and methodically outlining the procedure. The leader of the group can read through the steps to clarify any that are not understood. Members can then later, in their own time, practise the method.

At a subsequent group session, a discussion can take place on members' satisfaction or dissatisfaction with the method and any problems that may have arisen.

Women's Health Care Quiz

1) To help prevent cancer of the cervix a smear test should be done:

A. Every five years
B. Every ten years

Answer: **A** – *Every five years is the recommended period.*

2) To help prevent breast cancer you should examine your breasts:

A. Once every couple of months
B. Once a month

Answer: **B** – *Once a month, just after a period, or the same day each month if you don't have them.*

3) When the Menopause starts it means you are no longer fertile. True or false?

Answer: **False** – *The menopause progresses slowly, over a number of*

years and despite not experiencing a period for several months there can still be a possibility of pregnancy. A doctor can determine whether or not a woman remains fertile at this time.

4) Water retention, tiredness, cramps, mood swings and nausea are common symptoms of:

A. Vaginal infections
B. Cystitis
C. Premenstrual syndrome

Answer: **C** – *Premenstrual Syndrome.*

5) Painful periods are just something you have to put up with each month. True or false?

Answer: **False** – *There are many different ways of relieving the pain. Try exercise or a commercial preparation. If these don't work, see your GP.*

6) Every woman's menstrual cycle should last 28 days. True or false?

Answer: **False** – *This is an average figure. Many women have quite normal cycles of shorter or longer duration.*

7) A period occurs when an egg has not been fertilized by a sperm. True or false?

Answer: **True** – *The lining of the uterus is shed when fertilization has not occurred. This is a period.*

OBJECTIVES:

● To increase awareness of the need to practice birth control.
● To help individuals to make an informed decision when choosing a contraceptive method and improve understanding of effects on the body.
● To develop awareness of sexually transmitted infections.

Methods

There are several birth-control methods to choose from. There are more types of contraception for women than for men. Despite the progress which has been made in the last 20 years, the effectiveness of these methods in preventing pregnancy varies considerably and all have disadvantages as well as advantages. Each should therefore be carefully considered, in consultation with one's GP or family planning clinic if desired, before deciding which is the most suitable or before changing from one method to another. The following points may be helpful. The second, third and fourth points apply particularly to women who may wish to use the pill. Consider:

▶ Your lifestyle.
▶ Your age.
▶ Are you a smoker or non-smoker?
▶ Do you suffer from high blood pressure or heart disease?
▶ Do you have any particular feelings as to whether contraception should be the man's or woman's responsibility?
▶ Have you completed your family?

The Pill

For use by women, the Pill is an oral contraceptive. Pills are usually packaged in bubble packs with the day printed by each one so that it is easy to remember when to take them.

Types of Pill

There are several different types of Pill which vary slightly in hormone content and action. The most widely used are the **com-bined pills** which contain two hormones, oestrogen and progestogen. There are also Pills (sometimes called mini-pills) which contain progestogen only and no oestrogen. They are a little less reliable than the combined pills but they suit some women, especially those who are breast-feeding, or older women, who should avoid oestrogen-containing Pills.

How the Pill works

The combined Pill alters the hormone balance of the body so that no egg is released from the ovaries. The progestogen-only Pill does not always prevent ovulation but causes changes that make it difficult for sperm to enter the womb, or for the womb to accept a fertilised egg.

Advantages of the Combined Pill

▶ It is the most reliable reversible method of birth control.
▶ It does not interfere with sexual intercourse.
▶ It often relieves painful periods and may make bleeding lighter and more regular.
▶ It often relieves pre-menstrual tension.
▶ It can protect against some benign (non-cancerous) breast disease.
▶ It seems to reduce the risk of certain cysts on the ovary.
▶ It has a protective effect against cancer of the ovary and cancer of the womb, some pelvic infections and rheumatoid arthritis.

Side effects of Combined Pill use

Most women have few or no side effects at all. However there are some associated risks and these are listed below.

Nausea	Tiredness
Headache	Weight increase
Sore breasts	Depression

These effects usually disappear in a few months, but if they persist, a different type of Pill or alternative method of contraception may be suggested by the doctor.

Thrombosis is a blood clot which can form in an artery or vein, causing a blockage. This is serious and can be fatal causing a heart attack or stroke. Pill-users are at greater risk of developing a blood clot, but it is rare and the risk of getting it while on the Pill is very small. The risk of a stroke or heart attack is greater in diabetics, cigarette smokers and those with raised blood pressure. It is not advisable for women over 45 (and smokers over 35) to take the combined Pill. The risk of a stroke or heart attack increases with age. A woman whose family has a history of heart disease and/or thrombosis is advised not to take the Pill.

Blood pressure should be checked regularly by a doctor as the Pill tends to cause a slight rise in blood pressure.

Research is continuing into as yet unconfirmed studies showing that there might be a small increased risk of developing cancer of the breast or cervix in some women.

Advantages of progestogen-only Pill

This has fewer side effects than the combined Pill. There is less risk of blood clots and raised blood pressure.

Side effects of the progestogen-only Pill

There is a higher failure rate than the combined Pill. It also offers less protection against ectopic (outside the womb) pregnancy. This is uncommon but dangerous.

Depo-Provera

This is a hormonal contraceptive given by injection. It stops ovulation for three months by being released slowly into the body. It does not differ greatly from the progestogen-only Pill and has similar side effects. It is not commonly used, and is administered usually only to women for whom other methods have proved unsuitable.

The IUD (intrauterine device)

This is also known as an IUD, loop or coil and is an object about 1½″ in size made of plastic or plastic and copper wire which is inserted into the womb. It is left in the womb for two or more years depending on the type used (of which there are many). It is not really fully understood how an IUD prevents pregnancy and there are many theories.

An IUD makes sexual intercourse safe straight away and does not interfere in any way. The device usually has threads attached which hang down into the vagina so that a woman can check regularly that it is still in place. Occasionally an IUD can fall out. Pregnancies occur in IUD users when the IUD has been expelled, unknown to the user. The first year is the most common time for this to happen.

They are considered to be most suitable for women who have already had children. Although women without children can use them they are not a first choice. It is very reliable and non-hormonal. Of 100 women wearing an IUD, between two and four will become pregnant each year.

Side-effects of the IUD

Bleeding
Bleeding is common for the first couple of days after an IUD is fitted and may continue between periods for the first few months. Periods may be heavier than usual.

Pain
Cramp-like pain, similar to period pain or low backache is common shortly after a fitting and for a short while afterwards. Occasionally an IUD needs to be removed when a woman finds it very painful; otherwise pain is usually mild.

Perforation
Perforation of the womb by an IUD is a rare occurrence. Although it can cause pain, often there are no symptoms. Becoming pregnant, or not being able to feel the threads is often the first indication of perforation. The IUD no longer acts as a contraceptive as it is not in the right place. A small operation may be necessary to remove it.

Pelvic infection
IUD users are twice as likely to get a pelvic infection as Pill users. Any infection needs to be treated right away as it can impair fertility. Women with no children may wish to use an alternative method of contraception for this reason. It can be quite easily treated with antibiotics.

Barrier Methods

The Sheath
The Diaphragm
The Cap
Spermicides
The Contraceptive Sponge

The Sheath (Condom, French Letter, Protective)

Prevents sperm entering the vagina after ejaculation. It is made of thin rubber and is designed to be worn over an erect penis. It is the only reliable method for a man to use apart from sterilization.

The Diaphragm

This is a thin dome of rubber with a metal rim also covered in rubber. It covers the cervix and thus prevents sperm entering the uterus. It has to be used with a spermicide for it to be effective. A woman inserts it before intercourse. It needs to be left in for about six hours afterwards and then removed. It will last for about a year if properly cared for.

Caps

Smaller than diaphragms, these are made of rubber or plastic and are also designed to fit over the cervix. They are useful for women who cannot use a diaphragm. They must be used in conjunction with a spermicide, must be inserted before intercourse and not removed until at least six hours later.

Spermicides

Spermicides are chemicals which inactivate sperm. They are not reliable used on their own and should be used with a diaphragm or cap. They come in the form of creams, pessaries, jellies and aerosol foams.

The Contraceptive Sponge

This is a new barrier method for women. It is a sponge made of polyurethane foam impregnated with spermicide and has a loop attached to help remove it. It can be inserted any time before intercourse and is effective for 24 hours. It must remain in place for at least six hours after intercourse, and is then discarded. It appears to be less reliable than other barrier methods.

Sterilization

Sterilization should be thought of as a permanent method of birth control. Although there are operations to reverse the process they are not always successful. Most doctors, because of the permanent nature of the method, would wish to counsel the individual and sometimes the partner before a final decision is made, although legally, only the consent of the individual wanting the operation is required.

Male sterilization is a simpler process than that for females. Many GPs are trained to perform vasectomies and most operations require a local anaesthetic only. A vasectomy will not affect a man's sex drive physically or make him impotent and ejaculation will take place in the normal way. The only difference is that sperm will not be in the seminal fluid as the tube through which it passes, the vas deferens, has been blocked off.

There are several methods used for an operation for female sterilization, some require a general anaesthetic and others a local anaesthetic. All of them aim to block the Fallopian tubes to prevent an egg being fertilized by a sperm.

Menstrual cycles continue normally after sterilization although a few women find that their periods become heavier. A woman's sexual drive should not be affected by sterilization.

Coitus Interruptus (Withdrawal)

This requires the cooperation of both partners although it is one of the few male methods of birth control. No mechanical means are needed, the method simply requiring that the penis be withdrawn from the vagina just prior to ejaculation so that sperm do not enter. In this country it is the third most popular method of contraception.

Other Methods

Other natural methods involve working out the "safe period" in a woman's menstrual cycle – the period when pregnancy is least likely to occur. These methods are not as reliable as the Pill, coil, or barrier methods of contraception. The methods need practice, careful observation and record-keeping and abstinence from sexual intercourse at certain times of the month when the woman is likely to be fertile. For women who have irregular periods the "safe period" method is too unreliable as a method of birth control.

To work out the safe period these are the different methods:

The Temperature method

This relies on the measurement of normal changes in body temperature that occur after ovulation.

The Billings or Mucus method

This relies on the detection of changes in cervical mucus which occur near the time of ovulation.

The Calendar method

This involves working out your safe period in advance each month.

Combination Methods

Some people combine several methods in an attempt to be as safe as possible. This is often referred to as the double-check or sympto-thermal method.

Family Planning Services

Family planning services are provided free to everybody by the NHS and are available through GPs and family planning clinics.

GPs

An individual or couple wanting help with family planning do not have to go to their own GP for advice but can go to another doctor for this service. There are lists of GPs in libraries and ones who give advice on contraception have the letter 'C' after their names. A doctor is able to prescribe all contraceptives with the exception of condoms which are free only from clinics. All prescribed contraceptives are free.

Family Planning Clinics

All contraceptives are supplied free of charge. Some clinics help with subfertility and psychosexual problems. Most will do pregnancy tests and some offer pregnancy counselling.

The Brook Advisory Centres in London, Birmingham, Bristol, Coventry, Edinburgh and Liverpool provide free advice on birth control and supplies of contraceptives to young people. The Family Planning Association has some private clinics. Some provide vasectomy services only, others also provide general birth control and menopausal clinics.

How to find a local clinic

The address and times of the nearest clinic can be obtained from:
Health centres
Midwife
Hospital
Health Visitor
Telephone directory or Yellow Pages under 'family planning'

(This information contains extracts from material available from the Family Planning Association, Family Planning Information Service and Health Education Authority, and is reproduced here with their kind permission.)

Sexual Health Care

There are many infections which can be transmitted by sexual intercourse and the risk of contracting these is increased by having sexual intercourse with more than one partner or with someone who has had sexual relationships with more than one partner. It is not possible to rely on the presence of signs and symptoms to know if a person is infected as often no warning symptoms are present.

Some sexually transmitted infections and diseases include the following: urethritis, pubic lice, scabies, herpes genitalis, genital warts, gonorrhoea, syphilis and AIDS. The Health Education Authority provides leaflets on these conditions outlining the symptoms and treatment. It is impossible to diagnose and treat oneself. Special Clinics are available and should be contacted if:

▶ there is a possibility that someone you had sexual intercourse with recently has a sexually transmitted infection;

▶ you or your sex partner develop symptoms which are unusual for you, such as itching, soreness or discharge from the vagina, penis or anus;

▶ you develop a sore, lump or rash on the genital area, anus or mouth;

▶ you suffer from discomfort or increased frequency when passing water.

In these cases all sexual activity should be stopped and medical advice sought by either:

Consulting your GP

Some GPs are equipped to perform the necessary test and if not will refer you to a special clinic

or

Contacting your special clinic

These are clinics where free advice and treatment is available for sexually transmitted diseases by specially trained staff. No doctor's letter is needed and people of all ages can attend. These clinics have different names throughout the country. To find the location and opening hours of your local clinic either

▶ Ask your GP.

▶ Ask your Citizens Advice Bureau.

▶ Look in the telephone directory under Venereal Disease or VD.

▶ Look for notices or posters in public lavatories, health centres or post offices.

Using a sheath or condom reduces the risk of transmitting infection.

Aids

AIDS is a disease which can be sexually transmitted. It is caused by a virus for which there is no known cure at present. The virus, which can be present in body fluids, is detected via a screening test called the 'HIV Antibody Test' which traces the presence of antibodies. Using a sheath or condom reduces the risk of transmitting this or any other infection. On page 74 we have listed telephone numbers of organisations, all of whom have excellent published information freely available.

Contraception

DISCUSSION TOPICS:

● What do members consider to be the advantages and disadvantages of different contraceptive methods.
● What factors do they consider important in choosing a method.
● Pictures, films, posters and leaflets would help promote discussion of this subject. A speaker could also be invited to talk to a group and could perhaps, if appropriate, show members a range of contraceptives.

Sexually Transmitted Infections

▶ Obtain the number of your local Special Clinic and place it on your notice board or give it to members of the group in case of future need.

▶ Care must be taken when discussing this topic not to cause undue anxiety which could lead to the inhibition of a healthy and happy sex life. Some of these conditions are rare and most of them respond very well to treatment. The accent should be on the value of early intervention and the privacy, advice and service provided by the Special Clinics.

▶ Obtain a supply of the many leaflets available from your local Health Education Authority or in Scotland the Scottish Health Education Group. Participants could then take these away from the group and peruse them privately later.

▶ Films, slides and videos are also available which could be shown if appropriate.

OBJECTIVES:

- To promote awareness of the consequences of poor oral hygiene.
- To improve dental care.

Common Dental Problems

Tooth decay and gum disease are the two most common dental problems; the former occurs mostly in children and young adults. Gum disease takes hold more in later life in people over thirty. More teeth are lost through gum disease than for any other reason.

Dental Plaque

The main cause of both problems is plaque. This is the invisible layer of bacteria which coats the teeth and can be felt on them in the mornings even though they have been brushed the previous night. It contains large amounts of bacteria which grow on the teeth and gums and which are present in everyone's mouth.

Tooth Decay

If not removed, the bacteria in plaque combine with the food we eat, particularly sugar, and form acids. Acids attack and destroy the enamel covering of the teeth and then the dentine beneath. This is what is known as tooth decay.

Gum Disease

When bacteria infect the area around the teeth, gum disease results. If the gums bleed when brushed, it usually means that they have a mild form of gum disease called gingivitis, making them red, swollen and sore. If allowed to continue a much more serious disease – periodontitis – can develop, where progressive damage leads to destruction of the bone forming the tooth socket. If enough bone is destroyed the tooth will become loose and fall out.

A Prevention Plan

To prevent tooth decay and gum disease these steps need to be followed:

▶ Regular cleaning to remove plaque.
▶ Healthier diet.
▶ Regular dental check-ups

Regular Cleaning

The Brush. Effective brushing will remove plaque. The correct brush is essential. This should have a small head for reaching awkward areas of the mouth. It should have nylon tufts. Bristle tufts have hollow shafts and absorb water which softens them making them less effective. They may also harbour bacteria. A soft or medium brush will remove plaque just as well as a hard one but with less risk of damaging gums. Too hard brushing is a major cause of receding gums. The brush should be multi-tufted (lots of bristles) and have round-ended filaments. There is a British Standard (1979) BS5757 and many of the most well-known makes of brush conform to this. Brushes wear out quickly and should be replaced approximately every three months or they won't do their job properly.

The Toothpaste. Fluoride is known to make teeth less susceptible to tooth decay. Some water supplies contain fluoride – either occurring naturally or added by the Water Authority. Others do not. It is a good idea therefore to choose a toothpaste containing fluoride. A small blob is all that is needed.

The Brushing Technique

The Outside Surface. Apply the brush head at an angle of about 45 degrees and use a short back-and-forth brushing action. Pay particular attention to the gum margins where bacteria can be hidden. (The sides of the bristles are applied, not the tips.)

The Inside Surface. Clean the inside surface in the same way.

The Back Teeth. Brush the teeth right at the back of the mouth, especially the back edges of the last tooth in each row.

The Biting and Chewing Surfaces. Brush all these surfaces.

How to use dental floss

Dental floss is a thread made up of strong fibres which is used for cleaning the two surfaces between the teeth where the brush cannot reach, and for removing food debris. It feels rather awkward to use at first and needs perseverance but it is very effective at cleaning around the teeth. The waxed type may be a little easier to use for the beginner although some dentists maintain that the wax can be deposited on the teeth leaving a sticky area to which bacteria can cling.

A length of about 18 inches is easiest to manage. The ends are wrapped around the index fingers a couple of times. The floss is then pulled taut and eased gently between two teeth. It should be curled around the tooth to be cleaned and swept up and down between the gum and the biting surface. This action should be applied two to three times before repeating with the adjoining tooth. Continue to clean all upper and lower teeth in the same way.

Healthier Diet

Since the bacteria which do so much damage to teeth and gums multiply rapidly when they can feed on sugar, it makes sense to be more careful about one's diet, particularly sugar intake. Sugary foods – sweets, white or brown sugar, cakes, honey, biscuits and sweet drinks like orange squash or fizzy drinks – should all be reduced in the diet. It is preferable to have sweet things at meal times.

Ideally the teeth should be brushed clean after each meal, but this is not always possible. If snacks are eaten, it is better to eat foods which are sugar-free such as cheese, fruit, crisps, nuts or raw vegetables like carrot sticks. Artificial sweeteners can replace sugar in hot drinks.

Regular Dental Check-ups

There is no rigid rule as to how often it is necessary to visit the dentist. Some people's teeth are more susceptible to decay than others, for no apparent reason. The best thing to do is to ask the dentist how frequently a visit is needed.

The following list gives an indication of some of the different dental services available:

- ▶ Repairs to teeth and gums.
- ▶ Scaling.
- ▶ Polishing.
- ▶ Teaching correct home dental care including how to use cleaning items, correct brushing method.
- ▶ Advice on diet and nutrition.
- ▶ Orthodontics (straightening teeth).
- ▶ Construction of dentures.

Extra Help

There are other items you can buy which will also help in a prevention programme.

Dental Tape

Used in the same way as floss but this is a flat tape which beginners may find easier to use and kinder to sore gums.

Disclosing Agents

A disclosing tablet, when chewed, will show where brushing has not been thorough enough, by staining the remaining plaque on the teeth temporarily with coloured dye. It is a good idea to test one's brushing technique in this way for a week or two until it is effective at removing all plaque from the teeth at one go. It is still worthwhile to continue making checks about once a month.

Disclosing agents also come in liquid form. Red food colouring is a cheaper alternative and can be dabbed on with a cotton wool bud. All these dyes can stain clothes and so should be used with care.

Dental Sticks

These are not toothpicks but wooden sticks with a flattened tip. They are for removing plaque and should only be used if recommended by the dentist.

Interdental Brushes

These consist of one or more tufts to clean between teeth and they may be of particular help to someone with overlapping teeth, or who is wearing a fixed dental appliance.

Dental Mirror

A dental mirror can show the inside of the teeth where it is impossible to see with an ordinary mirror. It is particularly useful when used in combination with a disclosing agent, to see which parts of the inside of the teeth have not been brushed properly.

Other Dental Problems – Causes and Cures

Halitosis

More commonly known as "bad breath". Possible causes are:
► Poor dental hygiene.
► Untreated tooth decay.
► Smoking.
► Consumption of strong-smelling substances, eg garlic, onions, alcohol.
► Gum disease.
► 'Morning breath' – a tongue coated with bacterial organisms.
► Systemic changes elsewhere, eg stomach upset.
Mouthwashes, sprays and tablets are only effective, if at all, for a very brief period, by masking the smell.

Toothache

This may indicate that there is a cavity and that the pulp of the tooth is inflamed, or that an abscess has developed. The dentist should be contacted as soon as possible so that the problem can be diagnosed and treated. In the meantime, the pain can be alleviated somewhat by taking aspirin or a similar common pain reliever. If there is a cavity an old-fashioned but effective home remedy is to dip a very small ball of cotton wool into oil of cloves, squeeze it dry and then put it into the hole in the tooth. There are actual kits you can buy for this purpose which include the oil, cotton wool balls and a tiny pair of tweezers.

Sensitive Teeth

When a gap appears between the tooth and gum a small part of the tooth without the enamel to protect it may be sensitive to cold or hot or sweet things and cause discomfort. There are three reasons why this may have occurred:

► The gum may have receded due to extra hard brushing – perhaps the brush was too hard or it was used too forcefully. Clearly, a softer brush and more gentle brushing technique would prevent the problem from worsening, although once recession has occurred, gums cannot return to their former position.

► Lack of dental hygiene – plaque has built up along the gum line because teeth are not being cleaned regularly.

► Inefficient dental hygiene – teeth may be cleaned on a regular basis but a poor brushing technique is not removing the plaque.

Very often sensitivity will simply disappear. For persistent discomfort there are various remedies. Special toothpaste for this problem is available commercially. The dentist may also provide a special rinse or suggest other forms of treatment. It is important however to be sure that one's own dental care is regular and efficient.

Oral Hygiene for Dentures

Dentures need to be kept clean just as much as teeth. Plaque forms on dentures in the same way it forms on teeth and if it is not removed regularly will cause them to smell and taste unpleasant. There are three types of cleansers:

Abrasives
They are brushed on the denture like toothpaste. A soft or medium brush should be used and not too forcefully otherwise the polished surface could be rubbed away, making it easy for the dentures to become stained. Dentists can sometimes get dentures repolished if this has already happened.

Powders and Tablets
These are dissolved in water and dentures are then left to soak in the solution overnight.

Acid Cleaners
A weak acid solution is applied to the dentures and then after a brief period washed off.

A Dental Care Kit

The dentist may be able to provide a dental care kit. This would include such things as a toothbrush, dental mirror, disclosing tablets, fluoride toothpaste and dental floss. Kits can also be purchased from chemists.

A Dental First Aid Kit.

It is a good idea to keep a box or tin with a well-fitting lid containing items for use in emergencies. Or, include these items with the contents of a first aid kit:

▶ Small bottle oil of cloves
▶ One pair of tweezers
▶ Small pkt cotton wool
▶ 1 pkt painkilling tablets, eg aspirin

Dental Treatment and the NHS

Leaflets issued by the Department of Health (DoH) give general guidance on dental treatment on the National Health Service. Some of this information is reproduced here. Leaflets can be obtained at post offices or by writing to the DoH.

All NHS dental treatment is free if you are:

▶ Under 18 (except that you have to pay for dentures and bridges if you're over 16 and not in full-time education).

▶ A student under 19 in full-time education (if your education is not full time, or if you're 19 or over, you may be able to get free treatment on low income grounds).

▶ An expectant mother who was pregnant at the start of the treatment or who has had a baby in the last twelve months.

▶ In receipt of:
– Income Support
– Family Credit or are an adult dependent of someone who gets either Income Support or Family Credit

▶ Receiving free milk and vitamins and/or free prescriptions on grounds of low income. (If you're aged 16 or over, you can claim on your *own* low income grounds.)

▶ On a low income.

Everyone gets these things free:

▶ Repairs to dentures.

▶ Calling a dentist out of his surgery in an emergency.

▶ Home visits if necessary

(but in the last two cases, you will have to pay for any treatment given, unless you're entitled to free treatment).

How to get NHS treatment

If you cannot find a dentist through asking friends and neighbours, contact the nearest main post office, library, Community Health Council, Citizens Advice Bureau or Family Practitioner Committee, all of which have addresses in the telephone book, and ask to see the list of local dentists. When you have chosen a dentist, phone the surgery or go there to make an appointment. Say that you want NHS treatment. On the first visit and every time you start a new course of treatment, you must make sure that the dentist agrees to give you NHS treatment or you could be treated as a private patient.

> **Discussion Topics:**
>
> ● When did individual members last visit the dentist?
> ● What did the dentist do and how did they feel about the visit?
> ● Do they know what sort of condition their teeth/dentures are in now?
> ● What sort of oral hygiene routine does each person practise?

Self Disclosure

Provide each person with a disclosing tablet to chew and then let everyone see their teeth in a mirror to examine the areas covered by plaque. If possible, provide dental mirrors so that each person can also view areas awkward to see in an ordinary mirror.

In an optional additional exercise, each person then cleans their teeth and chews another tablet with the aim of identifying any deficiency in their brushing technique.

Oral Hygiene for Dentures

The different types of cleansers can be shown to individuals who wear dentures and the use of each described. They can try them out in their own time to see which they prefer.

Quiz

1) Apart from keeping them looking good, what is the main benefit of regularly keeping teeth clean?
A. To prevent 'bad breath'
B. To make your mouth feel fresh
C. To prevent tooth decay and gum disease

*Answer: **C** – Keeping teeth clean will prevent a layer of plaque from building up.*

2) What is the most common reason for gums bleeding when brushed?
A. Brushing too vigorously
B. Using too hard a brush
C. Gum disease

*Answer: **C** – A and B can cause bleeding gums, but the main reason is gum disease.*

3) Toothbrushes if used regularly wear out quickly and should be replaced on average:
A. Every month
B. Every three months
C. Once a year

*Answer: **B** – Replacing your toothbrush regularly is important or it will lose its effectiveness at cleaning.*

4) Certain foods are known to promote tooth decay. Which of the following three types of food is most damaging to teeth?
A. Honey
B. Artificial sweeteners
C. Crisps

*Answer: **A** – Sugary foods are destructive to teeth and should be avoided if possible.*

5) Gum disease, characterised by bleeding, swollen and sore gums can if allowed to continue lead to periodontitis. The result of this can be:
A. A visit to the dentist
B. Loss of teeth
C. Discomfort

*Answer: **B** – Because the bone holding the tooth is destroyed.*

6) A dentist should be seen:
A. When you have toothache
B. As frequently as the dentist advises
C. Once a year

*Answer: **B** – Ask your dentist how often you need to visit.*

7) The best kind of toothpaste to use for cleaning teeth contains:
A. Fluoride
B. Mint flavouring
C. Whiteners

*Answer: **A** – Fluoride helps prevent tooth decay.*

OBJECTIVES:
- To increase understanding of common faults and disorders of sight and methods of correction.
- To improve awareness of how to look after eyes.

Common Sight Faults

In Britain about one person in two uses glasses or contact lenses to compensate for imperfect eyesight. Often, visual handicaps occur because one or more parts of the eye are not functioning properly. Ageing can also affect vision – certain eye conditions tend to occur at different stages of life.

Most of us are familiar with the words used to describe common faults in sight or ocular disorders. We may be aware that we have a particular eye problem, but often our understanding of these terms is hazy. Without describing in detail the mechanisms of the eye, here is some clarification of common terms:

Short-sight (Myopia)

Distant objects are unclear. Near vision is often quite good. Glasses or contact lenses can compensate.

Long sightedness (Hypermetropia)

Near objects are unclear and although an unconscious effort will often correct focussing it can be tiring and cause headaches and strain. Glasses will correct the focus without the extra effort.

Astigmatism

Normally, the cornea is perfectly curved, like the surface of a ball. But a mis-shapen cornea is the cause of astigmatism and vision can be blurred or distorted. Other visual deficiencies may be present so that glasses may be prescribed to correct more than one fault.

Presbyopia

By middle age a person may find that reading is becoming progressively more difficult. A book may need to be held further away to avoid the print appearing blurred. This is because, with age, the elasticity of the lens is lost and consequently the eye's ability to change focus from near to far is reduced. Glasses will compensate in close work by giving the extra focussing power which the eye can no longer produce for itself.

Common Eye Disorders

Disorders of the eye can be revealed by an eye examination. The earlier the diagnosis is made, the better. An examination will often discover disease before the individual is aware of any symptoms. This is one reason why regular eye examinations are advisable.

Cataract

Cataracts are often associated with advancing age. Very often they do not interfere with vision enough to become troublesome. When vision does become affected, it is because the inside of the lens has become cloudy. When it becomes very cloudy, vision is badly affected and the lens will need to be removed in a surgical operation. This is a straightforward procedure which has an excellent chance of success in restoring vision. After the operation either a man-made lens will be implanted in the eye, or more commonly glasses will be prescribed.

Glaucoma

This condition results from abnormal pressure building up within the eyeball and thus restricting the supply of blood to the eye. It can develop quickly and painfully or slowly and insidiously.

The field of vision is progressively reduced, leading to blindness. The progression can be halted by medical treatment although the sight already lost cannot be restored. The chances of developing glaucoma at middle-age and over increase.

The Eye Examination

Good eyecare requires regular eye examinations and taking care of your glasses if you wear them. NHS eye examinations are subject to a charge set by the optician. The average price currently is between ten and fifteen pounds. Certain groups are exempt, including the following:

▶ Those in full-time education up to age 19;

▶ Children under 16;

▶ Those receiving Income Support;

▶ A person over 40 whose parent suffers from glaucoma as this condition can run in the family.

The purposes of having regular eye examinations are:

▶ To ensure and maintain an adequate standard of vision as far as possible;

▶ To avoid an early eye defect becoming permanent through neglect

▶ To see that the eyes are healthy;

▶ So that any general ailment affecting vision can be recognised as soon as possible;

▶ To check side effects of medical and other drugs.

Subsequent treatment could include:

▶ No prescription, but an examination later;

▶ A prescription for corrective lenses;

▶ The supply and fitting of contact lenses;

▶ Orthoptic treatment or eye exercises;

▶ Referral to the patient's family doctor;

▶ Referral directly to the Hospital Eye Service with a letter to the patient's GP;

▶ Ocular first aid.

Lenses

Spectacle Lenses

With the advent of the new laws introduced by the government in December 1984, most spectacles, with the exception of those prescribed for children under 16 and for people registered as blind or partially sighted, can be dispensed or sold by anyone, whether qualified and registered as an optician or not.

All glasses must be made up to exactly match your own prescription, although 'ready-made' glasses for reading are now allowed to be sold in this country.

Most glasses must now be paid for privately. Some people are still entitled to free NHS glasses, including children under 16, full-time students under 19 and anyone receiving Income Support.

Some high-power lenses, designed as 'complex' are available at subsidised charges on the NHS. A registered optician can advise you whether you qualify.

Types of Spectacle Lenses

Spectacle lenses can be made of glass or plastic or both. People who are very short-sighted or very long-sighted may have lenses which are thick and heavy. Thinner, lighter lenses are now available made of a new sort of "slimline" glass, called High Refractive Index Glass.

The larger the lenses, the thicker the glass has to be. Choosing a smaller frame will cut down the weight and improve the appearance of the spectacles.

Plastic lenses are half the weight of glass but are the same thickness. Plastic is tough and has a good resistance to impact so plastic lenses are particularly suitable for drivers.

Toughened lenses are slightly thicker than normal and are specially treated with heat to form a hard outer layer. They will crumble into relatively blunt-edged pieces when broken by a severe blow, and so are good for drivers.

Laminated lenses consist of two thin layers of glass interlaid with a wafer of plastic. If broken, the pieces of glass will adhere to the central layer of plastic; again these are ideal for drivers.

Anti-reflection coating can be applied to new lenses or a pair of glasses which has been worn for some time. It transmits more light – helpful for driving and reduces surface reflections so eliminating the 'glassy' look.

Tinted lenses reduce glare.

Photochromic glass lenses darken on exposure to sunlight and lighten indoors.

Bifocals/Trifocals/Multifocals

At around middle-age when the lens loses much of its flexibility and focussing on near objects clearly becomes more difficult, bifocals may be prescribed to improve close-range sight. In most cases, there are two different areas to a bifocal lens – the top part is usually used for distance and the lower part for reading and close work.

There are also trifocals and multifocals. These allow people to focus on objects in between far distance and near.

Contact Lenses

There are three main types of contact lens: corneal, schleral and soft (hydrophilic).

The Corneal Lens
This is a thin, round, saucer-shaped plastic disc. It can be 'hard' or 'gas-permeable'. The latter is more comfortable for some people to wear as it allows more oxygen to reach the eye.

The Schleral Lens
The first type of contact lens produced, this is now only used for special clinical purposes. It covers the whole of the visible eye, fitting inside the upper and lower lids.

The Soft Lens
This absorbs water and consists of 40% water and 60% plastic when in the eye. It has an average life of two years compared with six years or more with hard lenses. It can be worn for longer periods than hard lenses. Soft lenses may be used when swimming but *not* in chlorinated water.

Looking After Your Eyes

Do not watch TV in the dark. Look slightly down to the screen, not up at it and sit five feet or more away from it.

▶ Do close work in good light.

▶ If eyes feel sore and tired, soak clean cotton wool in a saline solution and place wet pads on the closed lids.

▶ Have your eyes professionally examined at least once every two years unless advised otherwise.

▶ Wash your glasses daily in warm soapy water. Dry on a soft cloth.

▶ When removing your glasses use both hands and take them off straight. Taking them off with one hand can make the frame loose or misaligned.

▶ Never look directly at the sun as this can damage the eyes.

▶ Do not rest glasses with lenses facing down on anything hard as they may become scratched. Make sure the lenses are facing upwards.

▶ Keep glasses in a spectacle case when they are not being worn.

▶ If you wear contact lenses ordinarily but keep a pair of glasses for emergency wear, make sure that your glasses prescription is kept up to date.

▶ Never clean plastic lenses when dry.

▶ If your glasses become loose have them tightened at an opticians. Do not attempt to do it yourself.

▶ Always hold your frames at the centre when polishing them and use a soft clean cloth.

▶ Wear good quality sunglasses. Distortions in lenses of cheap sunglasses can cause eyestrain and headaches.

(The Optical Information Council and the Association of Contact Lens Manufacturers kindly supplied some of the information presented here.)

DISCUSSION TOPICS:

● Any visual problems of members of group.
● Do any members who wear glasses know what sight fault they have and how their glasses are meant to correct the fault?
● When did members last have an eye test?
● How do individuals take care of their glasses/contact lenses?

Invite an optician to speak at a group session if possible. Demonstrate how to clean a pair of glasses.

OBJECTIVE:

● To increase awareness of the need for basic footcare and prevent foot problems arising.

Looking After Your Feet

Many foot problems can be avoided by paying attention to basic foot care. Prevent problems arising or stop problems already established from getting worse by following these tips:

▶ Make sure socks or stockings are the right size and not too tight.

▶ Don't buy shoes when in a hurry. Try both shoes on in the shop and walk a few paces in them to ensure they are comfortable and fit properly. Toes should have adequate space in which to spread. Do not buy shoes which have to be "broken in".

▶ Footwear should be appropriate to the occasion. For example, if your job requires you to be on your feet for much of the day, then flat, well-fitting and supportive shoes with a low or medium heel are the best choice.

▶ Footwear should be appropriate for the weather. Keep the feet and legs warm in winter by wearing woollen socks or stockings. Buy the type of boots which have warm linings, or wear two pairs of socks — as long as they are not too tight and restrict circulation. In hot weather, if you wear sandals, make sure they have straps to attach them properly to the foot. Shoes may be more comfortable in hot summer weather if they are worn half a size larger than usual.

▶ Cut nails regularly. After a bath is easiest. Do not allow them to get too long. Cut them straight across. Remove any rough edges with an emery board.

▶ Since shoes become shaped and moulded by the individual foot and no two feet are alike, secondhand shoes are best avoided.

Common Foot Problems

Here is a list of common foot problems, the causes and methods of prevention:

Ingrowing Toenails

Causes: Cutting the nail too far down. Wearing shoes that are too shallow and consequently putting pressure on the toes.

Characterized by: The toenail forced to grow into the skin resulting in a painful infection.

Treatment: Daily saline footbaths will help. However, professional assistance is usually needed for this problem as infection can set in and antibiotics and nail surgery are often necessary.

Prevention: Cut nails straight across, but not too short. Choose shoes which have adequate space for the toes.

Corns

Causes: Pressure or friction on a small area of the foot.

Characterized by: A thickened layer of skin.

Treatment: Emollient cream (rich handcream will do) should be rubbed in regularly to soften the area. Comfortable footwear that does not press on that particular spot should be worn. When the corn has been softened it can then be filed with an emery board. There are corn plasters available commercially. These are impregnated with acid and must be used with care for if they are worn too long they can worsen the problem.

Prevention: Choose well fitting shoes. Make sure that seams of socks, tights or stockings are not causing discomfort.

Bunions

Causes: Tight or short shoes. Tights, stockings or socks which are too short in the foot and pull back the big toe.

Characterized by: Deformity: the big-toe joint is pushed out of alignment and becomes stiff and rigid.

Treatment: Bunions usually require professional help, particularly where there is a marked degree of deformity. Hot footbaths may help relieve some of the discomfort and pieces of foam between the toes can help relieve the pressure. It is important not to aggravate the problem by wearing ill-fitting shoes.

Prevention: Well-fitting shoes and hosiery.

Verrucae

Causes: A viral infection of the skin.

Characterized by: Infectious warts on the feet.

Treatment: There are some quite effective remedies available commercially. These are usually in the form of lotions and ointments which are painted on a couple of times a day. They are recommended only if a person's general health is good. For individuals suffering from certain circulatory problems or diabetes they are contraindicated.

Prevention: Difficult to prevent as they are usually caught from other people, especially in swimming pools. However, washing the feet daily and drying properly between the toes may reduce the chance of infection.

Athlete's Foot

Causes: A fungal infection of the skin. Sweaty feet.

Characterized by: Itching and scaling between the toes or under the arch.

Treatment: Creams and powders are available commercially which are effective in treating this condition. Good hygiene will also reduce the hot, moist conditions in which this fungus will thrive. Cotton hosiery and shoes with leather uppers should be worn. In summer it helps to wear open sandals with no hosiery. Powder should be sprinkled in shoes as well as on feet for maximum effectiveness and any preparation should be continued for at least two weeks after the infection has cleared up.

Prevention: Daily washing and proper drying between the toes. It is preferable to wear shoes and socks made of natural materials.

Foot Hygiene

Wash feet at least once a day with soap and warm water. In hot weather, feet sweat more and may need washing more than once.

Dry feet thoroughly, especially between the toes where infections can arise. Dust between the toes with talcum powder.

Change into a clean pair of socks or tights each day. (For extra sweaty feet apply surgical spirit daily for two weeks using cotton wool or cotton wool buds.)

Footcare Products

There is quite a variety of commercial products available to help you take care of your feet. A few of them are described here. They can be purchased through chemists, some supermarkets and drugstores.

Foot Sprays

To cool and refresh tired or hot feet. This comes in an aerosol and can be sprayed directly on to the feet or through socks, tights or stockings. Anti-perspirants for the feet also come in aerosol form.

Foot Cream

Rubbed into the feet cream will cool them, help to keep them dry and fresh and reduce perspiration.

Chiropody Sponge

An alternative to pumice stone. This is an abrasive sponge, to be used with soap and water to remove rough skin.

Shoe Deodorising Spray

This makes any type of footwear odour-free when sprayed directly on to linings, for several months at a time.

Chiropody Services

Demand for chiropody services outstrips their availability and health authorities vary in what they provide. Although chiropody can be obtained through the NHS it is advisable to check with your own health authority whether you qualify. Each authority will usually have a service for priority groups. These include: pregnant and nursing mothers, school children up to age eighteen, the elderly (women over sixty and men over sixty-five), the mentally handicapped and the physically handicapped. Home visits may be provided for people who are housebound.

There are also chiropodists in private practice. The Citizens Advice Bureau, local library or telephone book will have a list of chiropodists.

Chiropodists have to undergo a three-year, full-time professional training to become state registered. However, the law allows people to practise chiropody without benefit of this training or state registration. A registered chiropodist may be recognised by these letters after his or her name, "SRCh" (State Registered Chiropodist) and "MChS" (Member of the Chiropody Society).

Footcare

Each person is asked to draw round one of their feet twice, so they have two pictures of the same foot. It is better if the drawing is made around the foot itself, but around the shoe will do. They are then asked to write on one of the drawings all the things about their feet they are dissatisfied with (and the other foot), eg. dry skin, corns, etc. After learning about basic footcare and preventive care, each person is asked to produce the other drawing and write on it the actions or methods necessary for improving their feet, eg. cut nails, etc.

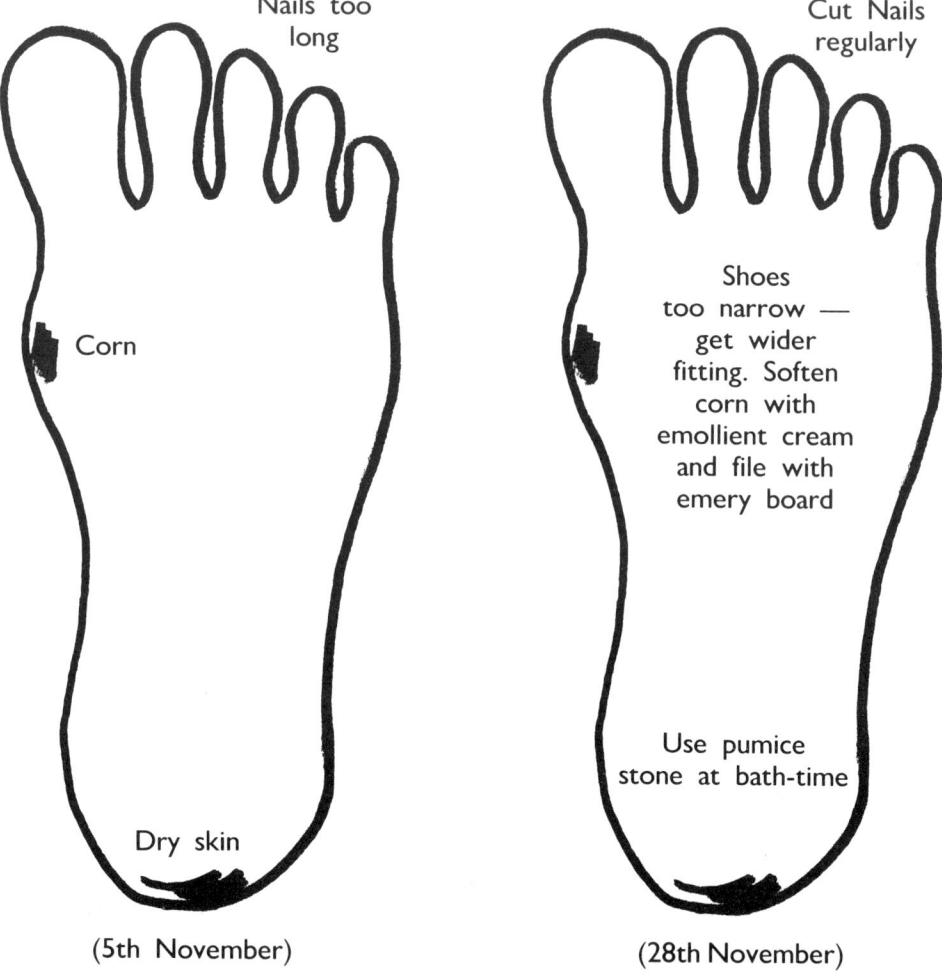

Nails too long

Corn

Dry skin

(5th November)

Cut Nails regularly

Shoes too narrow — get wider fitting. Soften corn with emollient cream and file with emery board

Use pumice stone at bath-time

(28th November)

▶ Invite a chiropodist to the group to talk about footcare.

Choosing Footwear

▶ Cut from magazines several pictures of shoes and boots. Ask members to rate each out of five (1 - low, 5 - high) for the following: comfort, fit, looks and durability. Ask members to identify what sort of occasions they would each be suitable for.

▶ Ask each person in turn to show others the shoes they have on and to say why they bought that particular pair, what they think of them now with regard to value for money, comfort, fit, looks and durability. Would they buy them again? If not, what would they buy?

Foot Exercise Routine

These exercises help revive tired feet and can be taught in group sessions. Ask members to follow these steps. Rest your legs on a chair and do the following:

▶ Point your toes down, then relax (repeat six times).

▶ Pull your toes back, then relax (repeat six times).

▶ Draw a circle in the air, first one way (repeat six times) then the other (repeat six times).

▶ With legs outstretched and feet pointing up, contract both sets of calf and thigh muscles, then relax (repeat six times).

Remedies for Tired Feet

½ lemon, cut in slices
1 bowl lukewarm water

Soak feet for 15 to 20 minutes. Rub any hard skin with the lemon slices, then rinse the feet in fresh water. Dust with talcum powder.

1 tablespoon mustard (or salt, or Epsom Salts)
1 bowl of very hot water

Soak feet for 10 to 15 minutes, then put them into a bowl of cold water. Rub vigorously with a towel until they are warm. Dust with talcum powder.

Foot Care Quiz

1) Athlete's foot is not infectious.
True or false?

Answer: **False** – *It is infectious. However it is most likely to occur in people who have very sweaty feet as it thrives in conditions of warmth and moisture. Regular washing and drying between the toes reduces the chance of the problem occurring.*

2) A pumice stone is used for filing toe nails.
True or false?

Answer: **False** – *It is used for removing rough skin on the soles and heels of the feet. It is most effective during a bath when the skin has softened in the water.*

3) There is no need to try both shoes on when buying shoes because both feet are the same size.
True or false?

Answer: **False** – *In most people one foot is slightly larger than the other. It is important to try both shoes on before buying them to be sure that they both fit well.*

4) Toe nails should be cut in a rounded shape.
True or false?

Answer: **False** – *They should be cut straight across. If they are cut in a rounded shape there is an increased risk of them growing into the skin.*

5) Secondhand shoes are not very good for the feet.
True or false?

Answer: **True** – *Everybody's feet are a different shape and when shoes are worn in they "mould" to the shape of that person's foot. Wearing somebody else's shoes can promote all types of foot problems.*

6) For good hygiene, feet should be washed every day.
True or false?

Answer: **True** – *More often if necessary in hot weather or if you suffer from sweaty feet.*

7) Corns are caused by pressure on a small area of the foot.
True or false?

Answer: **True** – *Tight shoes, ridges or seams can press on the skin. If this persists, the skin protects itself by forming a hard layer.*

8) Tights or socks should be changed about twice a week for cleanliness.
True or false?

Answer: **False** – *To prevent odour and decrease the risk of infection socks or tights should be clean each day.*

9) A pair of flat, floppy sandals would be the most comfortable thing to wear for someone who is on their feet all day.
True or false?

Answer: **False** – *A pair of floppy sandals will not support the foot. The heel of the sandals should be low or medium for maximum comfort.*

10) Buying shoes a half size too small is OK because they'll be broken in after they've been worn a few times.
True or false?

Answer: **False** – *Never buy shoes that are too small. They might get broken in but probably at the cost of developing one or more painful foot disorders.*

SECTION 2

PERSONAL APPEARANCE

OBJECTIVES:

● To increase awareness of the importance of clothing to personal appearance.
● To learn ways of improving appearance and thus promote positive self-image.

For the person working with a small budget, clothes should be chosen which can 'mix and match' with each other as much as possible so that a greater variety of outfits can be worn. Also, clothes which are properly looked after will look better, last longer and give better value for money.

Choosing Clothes

These points should be considered when shopping for clothes:

Lifestyle

Choose clothes appropriate for the occasions on which you plan to wear them. For example, a person who goes out to work in an office would probably be expected to look quite smart. At home more casual clothes could be worn.

Season

Buy clothes to suit the season – clothes which will keep you warm in winter and cool in summer. Some clothes can be worn all year round. A cotton shirt or blouse can be worn comfortably on a hot summer's day and beneath a sweater on a winter's day equally well.

Colour

Colour is a matter of personal taste and suitability, depending on hair colour and skin tone. To get the best use from a small wardrobe of clothes it is advisable to select colours which will co-ordinate, rather than choosing at random.

Body Shape

Some styles and patterns are more flattering to different body shapes than others.

Cost

Economies can be made when buying clothes without them having to look uninteresting or of poor quality. A cardigan bought for a very reasonable cost in a market can be made more interesting by replacing the buttons with a more distinctive set. Bargains can be found at jumble sales, car boot sales and second-hand shops.

Before buying an article of second-hand clothing it is advisable to examine it for moth holes, torn lining, stains, missing buttons or fading. It should only be purchased if it is in good condition or if there is a good chance of restoring faults. If it only costs a few pence it might be worth considering replacing the buttons with a new set, having it dry-cleaned or paying for it to be relined.

Sale time is a good time to go shopping for clothes although clothes should be examined carefully to ensure that a price reduction is not due to the item being damaged in some way.

Underwear

Underwear is worn for warmth and to improve the look of clothes. Thermal underwear is especially good for conserving body heat in winter and helps to reduce the risk of hypothermia particularly in elderly people. Vests can be worn for warmth, but white T-shirts can be more versatile as they can be worn both as vests *and* tops.

Fit

Wherever and whenever possible, always try on an article of clothing to ensure that it fits well and suits you. If unsure of your size, it is advisable to measure yourself with a tape measure and write down your measurements before leaving home. If you plan to buy something to go with something else, then wear it or take it along.

Fabrics

Fabrics are synthetic (man-made), natural or a blend of the two. Natural fabrics, such as wool or cotton wear well, feel comfortable and look attractive. They usually demand more care however than many synthetics or blends. Cost varies. Man-made fibres can often imitate natural fibres quite well, are usually machine-washable and often crease-resistant and quick-drying.

Footwear

Shoes should be carefully chosen so that the style is versatile. Although more expensive, leather is preferable to plastic material. It will last longer, look better and feel more comfortable. In the summertime canvas shoes or sandals can be worn. These are of course cheaper.

Accessories

Carefully chosen accessories can turn a plain outfit into a striking one. They can also turn a daytime outfit into appropriate wear for an evening out.

Take another look at the accessories you have. Can they be worn another way? Do you always wear a scarf round the neck with a knot at the front? A scarf can be worn in a variety of ways depending on size and length – hair tied back, round the waist, round the neck cravat-style, twisted together and pinned round a bun. A long strand of beads can be worn long, knotted 20's style or made into a double strand.

Men's accessories are rather more limited. A new tie could do wonders for a jacket though, or a new pair of cufflinks could dress up a shirt.

Clothes Maintenance

Look after your clothes and they will look after you. This means putting a little effort into their care. If clothes are not washed often enough the body grime which is absorbed becomes increasingly difficult to remove and can rot the fabric. If they are washed incorrectly they can be ruined and if stored incorrectly can become

creased or lose their shape. Ironing is still necessary for some fabrics unfortunately, particularly natural fabrics. There are right and wrong ways to iron and different temperatures for different fabrics. Clothes maintenance also means making minor repairs, giving garments a longer life.

Cleaning Methods

Clothes must now, by law, have labels which show the kind of fibre from which they are made. Many clothes also provide washing instructions. These will be shown by the use of a symbol and/or written instructions. The symbol will be part of the International Care Labelling Washing Symbols Code. There are five main symbols:

	Represents a wash-tub and tells you how to wash
	How to bleach
	How to iron
	Symbol for dry-cleaning
	How to dry

These are the basic symbols of the washing code but other information is usually included. For example:

	Means "do not", as in:
	do not iron

hand wash only

 The washtub shows temperature and washing time/agitation

The temperature is the recommended water temperature for the fabric to be washed. The washing times/agitation are Maximum, Medium (-) or Minimum (--). Here is the complete Code.

Machine Washing

▶ Use the right type of washing powder in the correct amount. Too much powder will not rinse out, too little makes the wash grey.

▶ Use the correct washing programme. Shrinkage, fading, bleeding of dyes, stretching or yellowing can all be the result of incorrect machine washing.

▶ Do not over-stuff the machine. The washing will not circulate properly and consequently will not be cleaned adequately. Do two loads instead.

▶ It is better to stick to one fabric group when doing a wash although mixed loads can be washed also. Set the programme to correspond to the article in the load with the lowest wash temperature.

Hand-washing

▶ Hand-wash delicate fabrics, wool and non-colourfast fabrics.

▶ Dissolve powder completely in warm water before doing the wash.

▶ Use one of the special commercial products for washing wool.

▶ Always dry woollen clothes flat to keep their shape.

Sorting the Wash

▶ Make sure all items are removed from pockets, eg coins (which can damage machines), paper handkerchiefs, bus tickets, etc.

▶ Do up all zips, buttons, and other fasteners. They can be damaged or damage other articles.

▶ Loosely tie ribbons, apron strings, etc.

▶ Repair tears, secure loose buttons.

▶ Treat stains before washing.

▶ Sort clothes according to wash code and separate whites and coloureds.

SUMMARY OF WASHING SYMBOLS

Symbol	Washing Temperature		Washing Time/ Agitation	Rinse	Spinning/ Wringing	Fabric	Benefits
	Machine	Hand					
95	very hot 95°C to boil	hand-hot 50°C or boil	maximum	normal	normal	White cotton and linen articles without special finishes	Ensures whiteness and stain removal
60	hot 60°C	hand-hot 50°C	maximum	normal	normal	Cotton, linen or viscose articles without special finishes where colours are fast at 60°C	Maintains colours
60	hot 60°C	hand-hot 50°C	medium	cold	short spin or damp dry	White nylon; white polyester/cotton mixtures	Prolongs whiteness — minimises creasing
50	hand-hot 50°C	hand-hot 50°C	medium	cold	short spin or damp dry	Coloured nylon; polyester; cotton and viscose articles with special finishes; acrylic/cotton mixtures; coloured polyester/cotton mixtures	Safeguards colour & finish – minimises creasing
40	warm 40°C	warm 40°C	maximum	normal	normal	Cotton, linen or viscose articles where colours are fast at 40°C, but not at 60°C	Safeguards the colour fastness
40	warm 40°C	warm 40°C	minimum	cold	short spin	Acrylics; acetate and triacetate, including mixtures with wool; polyester/wool blends	Preserves colour & shape – minimises creasing
40	warm 40°C	warm 40°C	minimum do not rub	normal	normal spin do not hand wring	Wool, including blankets, and wool mixtures with cotton or viscose; silk	Keeps colour, size and handle
30	cool 30°C	cool 30°C	minimum	cold	short spin do not hand wring	Silk and printed acetate fabrics with colours not fast at 40°C	Prevents colour loss
95	very hot 95°C to boil	hand-hot 50°C or boil	minimum	cold	damp dry	Cotton articles with special finishes capable of being boiled but requiring damp drying	Prolongs whiteness, retains special crease resistant finish
(tub with hand)	DO NOT MACHINE WASH						
(crossed tub)	DO NOT WASH						

WASHING TEMPERATURES

100°C	Boil	Self-explanatory.
95°C	Very Hot	Water heated to near boiling temperature.
60°C	Hot	Hotter than the hand can bear. The temperature of water coming from many domestic hot taps.
50°C	Hand-hot	As hot as the hand can bear.
40°C	Warm	Pleasantly warm to the hand.
30°C	Cool	Feels cool to the touch.

Dry Cleaning

Dry cleaning is expensive and best avoided if your budget is limited. Some launderettes have coin-operated dry-cleaning machines which work out cheaper although some types of clothing should not be cleaned in a coin-op machine.

  **These symbols mean that a coin-op machine should not be used.**

  **These symbols mean that a coin-op machine or professional dry cleaners can be used.**

Clothes Care Products

Detergents

These clean clothes. They come in liquid form, powder or flakes and are designed to do different jobs. They all give directions for use and for which fabrics they are most suitable.

Fabric Conditioners

These soften fabrics, reduce static and cling and reduce creases. They are particularly suitable for woollens and towels. Liquid conditioner should be diluted before pouring it into the rinse water when washing by hand.

Pre-wash Products

These help to remove stains in the wash and are applied to garments before putting them in the machine.

Household Bar Soap

For heavily soiled clothes. Heavily soiled areas of clothing, such as shirt collars, can be dampened and rubbed gently with soap before being washed.

Stain Removal

Treat stains before washing clothes and ideally as soon as they occur. It is cheaper to stop a stain setting by either sponging it or soaking it as quickly as possible in cool water rather than using a pre-wash programme on a washing machine. Never use hot water on a stain as it will set.

Drying Clothes

Tumble drying is very costly and it is best where possible to dry clothes on a line. Indoor drying on wet days can be done on a clothes horse or on a line hung in the bathroom. Special racks are also available which hook on to radiators.

Ironing

These are the symbols for ironing:

Temperature suitable for these fabrics

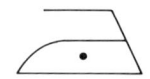 **Cool (120°C) Polyester, nylon, acrylic, triacetate, acetate**

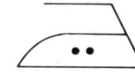 **Warm (160°C) Wool, silk, polyester mixes**

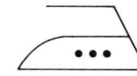 **Hot (210°C) Linen, cotton, viscose, rayon**

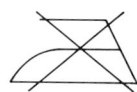 **Do not iron**

With modern irons, it is simply a matter of matching the dots found on the controls to the dots on the garment label. Older irons may have other types of controls. These may have fabric types written on – cotton being the hottest and silk the coolest.

Guidelines for ironing

▶ It is easier to iron out creases if the washing is damp. A steam iron will do the same job. Other methods are to spray clothes with water from a plant spray, or iron on a damp cloth placed over the item.

▶ It is better to iron seams or hems on the wrong side of the fabric to prevent a line showing through.

▶ Iron acetates or triacetates on the wrong side otherwise they will go shiny.

▶ Do not iron over buttons or other fastenings including zips.

▶ Clothes can be starched with an aerosol while ironing.

Everyday Storage

▶ Store sweaters in drawers after neatly folding them. Hanging them up will make them lose their shape.

▶ Anything which has been dry-cleaned should be hung in fresh air or a well ventilated room for a few hours before putting it away to get rid of toxic fumes.

▶ A wardrobe should not be over-full as creasing will occur.

▶ Jackets, coats and clothes made from heavy fabrics should be hung on sturdy wooden or plastic hangers rather than thin wire hangers so that they keep their shape.

▶ Skirts and trousers should be hung on hangers with clips.

▶ To keep socks in pairs put a pair together and roll the top of one back over both.

▶ Make up bags of lavender or other sweet-smelling herbs and put them in clothes drawers.

▶ Store dirty clothes away from clean clothes in a clothes basket. To prevent snagging of clothes if you have a wicker type of basket line with a plastic bag.

Mending

Basic repairs or alterations to clothes such as sewing on a button, darning a sock or lowering a hem need to be taught by another person. Reading a book is not the best way to learn. There are many products which will provide short cuts however and certain points to take note of to ensure success.

▶ Always mend tears or holes as soon as possible to avoid them getting worse and looking unsightly when mended.

▶ Use a colour of wool or thread close to the colour of the type of clothing being mended so that the mend will not be noticeable. It may be possible to unravel some threads from the item to use.

▶ When sewing on a button, use button thread if possible. This is thicker and stronger than ordinary thread. If ordinary thread is used, it should be doubled for extra strength.

▶ It is a good idea to keep scraps of fabric from anything one has made oneself for patching with.

▶ Iron-on patches can be bought commercially but it may be difficult to find one which will be a suitable match in colour and pattern.

▶ Use iron-on hemming tape for altering hems on skirts or trousers. This is effective, convenient and helps avoid crease lines.

▶ Men's jackets can be patched with leather patches, available commercially, if the elbows become worn. They must be removed for dry-cleaning however.

▶ Keep a "mending plait" in a sewing kit. It comes in two types. One is of many different brightly coloured threads for making small repairs to clothes and the other is of brown shades for repairs to stockings and tights.

▶ Darning wool can be purchased in several different colours wound on to a card.

A Basic Sewing Kit

▶ Sewing plait (bright colours)
▶ Card of darning wool
▶ Packet of assorted needles
▶ Box of pins
▶ Small pair of sharp scissors

Extras

- ▶ Tape measure
- ▶ Range of different-coloured cotton threads
- ▶ Hemming tape
- ▶ Darning mushroom
- ▶ Card of shirt buttons
- ▶ Seam ripper
- ▶ Hooks-and-eyes and press studs
- ▶ Tailor's chalk
- ▶ Reel of tacking cotton

Shoe Care

Take care of shoes by polishing them regularly. Shoes made of leather need more care than those made of synthetic materials. Leather needs "feeding" with wax polish to keep it soft and supple and looking good. The wax will also waterproof the shoes to some extent. Shoes made of synthetic materials are cheaper, waterproof (unless water seeps in through poor seams and joins) and do not require as much looking after. Synthetics however do not stretch like leather and often do not last as long.

How to Polish Shoes

- ▶ First remove all dust and dirt with a brush.
- ▶ Do not polish shoes if wet – wait until they have dried naturally. (Never dry leather shoes using direct heat, in front of an open fire, for example, as they will dry hard.)
- ▶ Choose the right shade of polish to match shoes.
- ▶ If applying liquid wax, simply dab sponge applicator on shoe and spread polish using light strokes. The polish will dry to a shine without requiring any buffing.
- ▶ If applying ordinary wax polish, use a cloth to rub well into the leather.
- ▶ Buff up by brushing with a soft brush.
- ▶ Rubbing gently with a soft cloth will bring up a shine.

DISCUSSION TOPICS:
● What does the term "personal appearance" mean to different people?
● Is personal appearance important? What do clothes make people feel about themselves?
● Do we always see ourselves as others see us?

Interview/Party

Each person is given a sheet of paper with "Interview" written at the top left-hand side and "Party" on the other side. Members should write down what is appropriate dress, grooming and hygiene for each setting. People's choices are then discussed as a group. Interview or party can be substituted with other social settings, and should be chosen to be relevant to the members of the group.

Life-drawing

The group is split into pairs. Lengths of drawing paper should be stuck on the walls around the room with about 30cms (1 foot) of paper resting on the floor. One person from each pair should remove their shoes and stand on the paper and rest against the wall facing outwards. Their partner draws round them with a pencil. They then move to a new piece of paper and swap over. Each person should then have an outline drawing of themselves. On the drawing, they can use any medium they like – crayon, paint, felt-tip pen, collage, etc – to colour in the figure. They should denote things they like about themselves and things they feel they need to work on. It should be made clear that the purpose of this exercise is not to examine personal qualities but to focus on anything relating to personal appearance. If necessary, a list of specific areas should be provided, eg nails, hair, complexion, clothes etc. It may help to give a time limit, eg half an hour, in which to complete the drawing.

Discuss people's drawings during the second half of the group. Another way of achieving the same result, self-assessment of personal appearance, is to provide each member with a sheet of paper similar to the one given below. Each person then fills it in in a given time.

Personal Appearance

NAME: _____   HAIR COLOUR: _____

WEIGHT: _____   HEIGHT: _____

AGE: _____   COMPLEXION: _____

Positive Attributes	Things I'd Like to Improve
1.	1.
2.	2.
3.	3.
4.	4.
5.	5.

It is not uncommon for people to have a much longer right-hand column. When this occurs, the help of the group can be solicited in contributing to each other's list of positive attributes.

This form can be filled in at the beginning of a number of planned group sessions. It can be produced again in the last session and members asked to draw up a third column entitled "I can improve this by . . ." The member is asked to then write a statement of action by each of the comments in the "Things I'd like to improve" column. Here is an example of how part of a form would look:

Personal Appearance

NAME: John Jones   HAIR COLOUR: Dark Brown

WEIGHT: 14st 10lbs   HEIGHT: 5'11"

AGE: 42   COMPLEXION: Good colour, clear

Positive Attributes	Things I'd like to Improve	I can improve this by:
1. Neat & tidy appearance	1. Overweight	1. Seeing my doctor & going on a low calorie diet to lose 2 stone.
2.	2. Bite nails	2. Stop biting nails – paint nail biting solution on each day to remind me.
3.	3.	3.
4.	4.	4.
5.	5.	5.

Buying Clothes

DISCUSSION TOPICS:

- Where do individuals shop for their clothes: retail outlets, Oxfam, markets, jumble sales, etc? What are the advantages and disadvantages of each?
- How do individuals budget for clothes?
- How do they plan for what they need?
- Do they buy something with the rest of their wardrobe in mind?
- Do they buy on impulse?

Prioritizing

What are individual priorities when buying clothes? Provide each person with a piece of paper with an identical list written on it as below:

Colour	Fashionable
Size	Washability
Price	Durability
Fabric	Co-ordination with other clothes
Fit	Other

Each person is asked to number the factors in order of importance to them. The list can relate to the purchase of clothes generally or a specific item can be suggested, eg winter jacket. Lists should then be discussed by the group, examining people's choices.

Selecting a wardrobe of clothes

Group members are asked to look through old magazines and make up a wardrobe for themselves by selecting pictures of clothes that appeal to them. Each person should paste the pictures on a piece of paper so that individual efforts can be shown to the group and discussed. Discussion could include co-ordination of styles, colour, compatibility with lifestyle, etc.

An alternative would be to prepare pictures beforehand by cutting them out and sorting them into boxes, eg coats, shoes, accessories, etc. Group members could be asked to select an item from each box to make up a single outfit. The discussion should follow the same lines.

Best Dressed People

Every year there is a list of the world's ten best-dressed women. The group are asked to each individually write down the names of the people they would choose and why. If it is a mixed group, an alternative could be "the ten best-dressed people". Another title could also be the "five best and five worst-dressed".

People Pictures

Cut out full-length pictures of people, famous or not, from magazines and mount them on single pieces of card. Discuss how group members feel about what they are wearing.

The Cost of Clothes

This exercise can help those who are not really in touch with today's prices become more aware of how much clothes cost. It can be followed up with a visit to a local store or stores. Comparisons of prices can be made. A visit to an Oxfam or other similar shop could also take place.

A range of preferably new or fairly new clothes should be displayed on hangers, ideally hanging from a rack. There are then two options:

a) Have a "price tag" made up for each item showing the true original purchase price. The prices should all be displayed on a table. Each group member is asked to match a price tag and the item of clothing it corresponds with.

b) The clothes and price tags are displayed in the same way. Each person is asked to write down which items and prices correspond on a piece of paper.

Discuss people's choices and what the correct prices are. This is an exercise which can precede a general discussion about the prices of clothes.

Accessories

Collect a number of different types of accessory together – beads, brooches, earrings, scarves, belts, cufflinks, tiepins, etc. Display one accessory at a time to the group and ask members to demonstrate a way of wearing it. For example, a brooch can be worn at the neck of a blouse, on the collar, on a lapel, on a dressy scarf. How many ways can members think of? Some accessories can only be worn in one way, eg cufflinks, tie-pins. Members could try these on to see how they look, particularly if they are not in the habit of wearing them.

Identifying clothes which suit oneself

Provide each person with a piece of paper which has a line drawn vertically down the middle. The left column should read at the top "Clothes which suit me" and the right column "Clothes which don't suit me". Each person is then given five to ten minutes to list clothes in each column. Individuals then take it in turns to read out their lists to the group and explain their choices.

Personal size record

Each member, with the aid of a tape measure and assistance from the leader if necessary, takes their body measurements and records them in both inches and centimetres on a sheet of paper. This may then be kept as a personal size record.

Clothes Maintenance

DISCUSSION TOPICS:

● How do group members keep their clothes clean? Include discussion of washing methods, use of clothes brushes, stain removers, polishing of shoes, etc.
● When clothes need repairs what do members do about it?

Washing clothes

On a blackboard illustrate the following: (excluding the words on the right)

	MACHINE	HAND WASH
50	Medium wash in synthetics cycle	Hand-hot
	Cold rinse. Short spin or damp dry	
(triangle crossed out)	Do Not Use Chlorine Bleach	
(iron with two dots)	Warm	
(circle with P)	May be dry cleaned	

This represents a clothes label. Discuss the meaning of symbols, asking members to fill in the missing words. This exercise could be continued by changing the symbols each time.

Mending

Ask each group member to write a list of items they would consider necessary for a basic sewing kit for mending and repairs. When each person has completed their list, discuss how they would use the items.

Provide each member with squares of material and a button to sew on.

Demonstrate the method and ask each member of the group to follow and practice. The more able members can help those who are less able. Other basic sewing methods can be taught in this way until members are confident enough in their sewing ability to attempt repairs of clothing.

Storage

Provide a number of different kinds of clothing. Provide different types of hangers and if possible, drawers and a wardrobe, or cupboards with a clothes rail. If it is not possible, substitute a table. Ask each member to pick up an article of clothing in turn and demonstrate how it should be hung or folded and stored.

Other things to teach

▶ Teach how to remove stains by, for example, pouring cold tea on an article and using the appropriate methods of stain removal.

▶ The best way to teach the use of a washing machine and tumble dryer, hanging clothes out to dry, etc is to provide a practical step-by-step demonstration and let the group members actually undertake the particular activity themselves.

▶ A visit to a launderette to do a wash might be of assistance to some group members.

▶ Ironing is also best taught by demonstration and practice. The person demonstrating can show how to iron one section – a sleeve for example, and the learner can then try ironing the other sleeve and so on.

Clothes Maintenance Quiz

1) What is bleach used for?
A. To whiten fabrics and remove stains
B. To make towels soft
C. To make ironing easier

*Answer: **A** – It is essential to follow the directions correctly when using bleach as it can rot fabric.*

2) Why do ironing boards have a rounded end?
A. So you don't accidentally hurt yourself on sharp corners
B. To make ironing awkward shapes easier.
C. No particular reason – it's just a traditional shape

*Answer: **B** – For example shoulders on shirts are easiest to iron if draped over the rounded end.*

3) This is a common symbol you see on garment labels or washing machines. What does it mean?
A. It refers to garments made of wool
B. White cottons
C. Minimum iron

*Answer: **A**.*

4) You have just hand-washed a woollen sweater. How would you dry it?
A. Hang it on the line
B. Hang it over a warm radiator
C. Lay it out flat

*Answer: **C** – Woollen clothes should never be hung as they will stretch out of shape.*

5) You have just finished doing a mixed wash and have discovered

that a couple of garments have shrunk and will no longer fit. This is because:

A. The washing water was too hot
B. The washing water was not hot enough
C. The washing was washed for too long

Answer: **A** *– The temperature of the water in a mixed wash should correspond to the item of clothing requiring the lowest wash temperature.*

6) Biological powders are particularly good for:

A. Washing woollens
B. Hand washing
C. Removing protein stains

Answer: **C** *– Stains such as egg and gravy.*

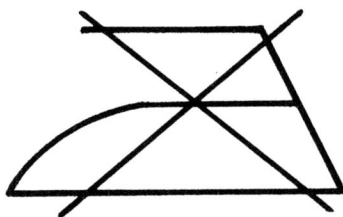

7) What does this symbol represent?

A. Do not iron
B. Cool iron recommended
C. Minimum iron

Answer: **A.**

8) To safeguard colour fastness it is essential with some garments that the wash temperature is:

A. Boiling
B. Fairly high
C. Low

Answer: **C** *– Low temperatures safeguard clothes coloured with unstable dyes.*

OBJECTIVE:

● To improve awareness of the need for personal hygiene and encourage good personal habits.

A daily bath is ideal for cleanliness. If bathing each day is not possible, then a thorough wash should be substituted to wash away bacteria and dirt.

Bathing can also be good in other ways – for cosmetic or therapeutic value or for relaxation.

Showering is supposedly a healthier way of cleansing the body as the dead cells and dirt are washed off straight away. The water spray also aids circulation.

Bathing Basics

For a bath you will need soap, flannel and towel. The towel and flannel should be changed regularly. There is a wide range of soaps on the market to choose from. Transparent glycerine soaps are good for sensitive or dry skins; medicated soaps are for very greasy or spotty skins. Anti-bacterial soaps have a deodorising action. Super-fatted soaps moisturise dry skin. There are many others available, including the liquid soaps, and prices vary considerably.

Bath Aids

Pumice Stone

A small block of volcanic rock which is used to rub off hard skin from feet and elbows. It is used in a gentle, circular motion while bathing.

Loofah

This is a vegetable gourd with a rough texture. It is bought flat but expands in warm water. It is rubbed over the skin – particularly the back – to improve circulation, and remove dead skin cells.

Back-brush

A brush on a long handle used in the same way as a loofah.

Bath Additives

Bath oils, bubble baths, bath salts and other additives can be added to the bath water. They have various functions – for cleansing and moisturising the skin or softening the water.

They can be purchased from shops or made at home more cheaply from ordinary ingredients.

Personal Freshness

A deodorant does not reduce perspiration but simply kills the bacteria which cause body odour.

Most deodorants now include anti-perspirants which as the name implies, actually reduce perspiration as well as acting as a deodorant.

There are two main types of deodorant/antiperspirant – roll-ons and aerosols. Both are convenient and it is really a matter of personal choice as to which is preferred. They can be perfumed or non-perfumed. Refills can be bought for the roll-on type and this works out cheaper. Occasionally a product will cause an allergic reaction – usually a sensation of itching or burning. This can happen even if the product has been used for some time without any adverse reaction. The best solution is to avoid using any product for a few days and then to change to another.

Guidelines for Maintaining Personal Hygiene

▶ Wear fresh clothes daily, in particular underwear, socks, tights or stockings. These are worn close to the body and will therefore absorb the body's moisture. The moisture decomposes when attacked by bacteria, causing an unpleasant odour.

▶ Bath or wash thoroughly every day, paying special attention to hands, underarms, feet and the genital area.

▶ Keep flannels clean or the bacteria which develop can cause skin infections. This is especially important for those with greasy or spotty skins.

▶ Change towels regularly.

▶ Use a deodorant/anti-perspirant daily.

Feminine Hygiene

The monthly period – menstruation – is a natural function. This is a time when extra attention should be paid to personal hygiene. It is important to keep a stock of sanitary towels or tampons ready in drawer or cupboard. There are many different types on the market. Some women prefer one to the other. Both are effective if changed regularly. Some women experience a particularly heavy flow for the first day or two of a period; this often tapers off towards the end. There are tampons and towels made specially for this which are more dense and therefore more absorbent. Some women find tampons are more hygienic because they are inserted into the vagina. They are also a little easier to dispose of as they can, along with the cardboard applicator, be flushed down the toilet.

There used to be an old-wives' tale that said you should not have a bath during your period. This is untrue and in fact personal hygiene at this time is even more important than usual.

Because of the personal nature of this component of self-care a single-sex group is advisable.

Assessing the effectiveness of individuals' personal hygiene routines and teaching some aspects of the subject may be more appropriate *before* commencing the group sessions. Teaching one-to-one may also be considered as a preferred alternative.

Washing (Pre-group and for assessment)

Provide each person with a sheet of paper with a drawing of a figure on it, facing front and back as shown. The person is asked to shade in the areas of the body which he/she washes at least once a day. This will assist the person organising a group in knowing what the needs are of individual members when teaching them about hygiene.

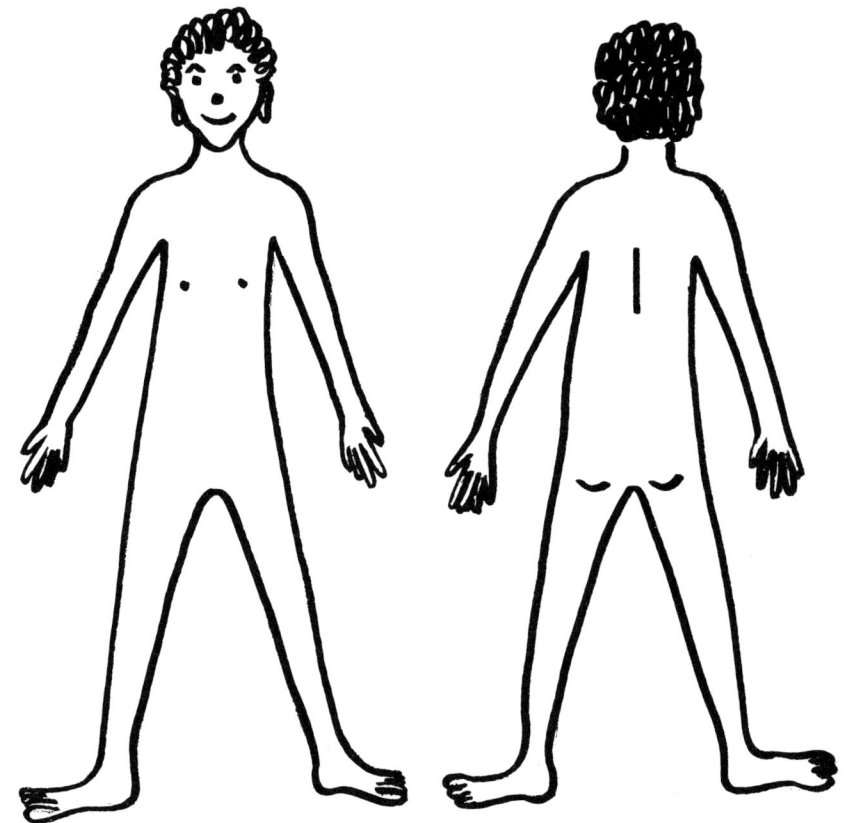

Sponge-bag

Draw a sponge-bag on a blackboard. Ask group members to imagine that they are going on holiday for a week and to put all the toilet requisites they need into their sponge-bag. What would they take? Each item suggested is written inside the drawing of the sponge-bag:

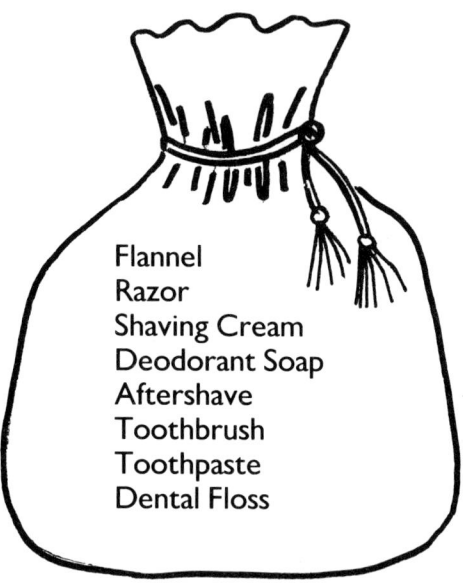

Flannel
Razor
Shaving Cream
Deodorant Soap
Aftershave
Toothbrush
Toothpaste
Dental Floss

Discuss the items suggested and why they have been chosen.

Variation 1

Demonstrate basic items necessary by using a real sponge-bag and real items.

Variation 2

Make a large outline drawing of a sponge-bag on paper. Ask members to look through magazines to find pictures to cut out of aids to personal hygiene. Stick inside the sponge-bag.

Variation 3

Each person is provided with an outline drawing of a sponge-bag and is asked to write in basic personal care items. After a short time individual choices can be compared and discussed.

OBJECTIVE:

● To identify different types of hair, the special needs of each type and promote effective methods of caring for hair.

Types of Hair

Normal Hair

Characteristics: Looks clean and shiny and has body and bounce.

Greasy Hair

Characteristics: Lank and lifeless and often dirty-looking because it attracts dust and grime. This is because too much oil is produced by the glands in the scalp.

Dry Hair

Characteristics: Looks dull and lacks shine. May be difficult to manage. It is easily damaged, giving rise to split ends and broken hair-shafts. Harsh treatments, eg strong perms, bleaches, very hot hairdryers, contribute to damaging the hair.

Basic Equipment

Combs and Brushes

Deciding whether to use a comb or brush is really a matter of personal choice. Combs are cheaper but brushes are more versatile. The best type of comb to buy is one with different sized teeth at each end. The wide teeth should be used to comb it out when wet when it is stretchy and vulnerable to being pulled or weakened. The narrow teeth can be used on dry hair.

Brushes can be bristle or plastic as long as the "bristles" have rounded ends and are not too hard on the scalp. Some brushes are shaped to style the hair while it is being dried with a hairdryer.

Cleaning Combs and Brushes

It is important to keep combs and brushes clean. They should also never be lent to other people to use. Warm soapy water (using shampoo or washing up liquid) should be used for cleaning. To clean a brush, first draw a comb through it to remove the hair that has collected in it. Both comb and brush should then be thoroughly cleaned in the water. A nailbrush can be used to scrub the teeth of the comb or brush bristles gently to remove accumulated grease and dust. Leave the brush to dry naturally on a towel with the bristles facing downwards. A comb can be dried with a towel.

Drying and Styling Equipment

Hairdryers

Hairdryers come in all shapes and sizes. The best type to have is small and light so it is easy to hold, and not overpowering as too hot a dryer will damage hair.

A dryer should not be used too close to the hair and should be moved briskly over the hair when drying, rather than concentrating too long on one area. A lot of dryers have attachments to style the hair as well as to dry it.

Curling Tongs

These can damage the hair if they are used too hot or too often but can be particularly useful as a quick method of styling hair. Some incorporate steam and are more gentle on the hair.

Heated Rollers

Like tongs, heated rollers are a quick way of styling hair. Although some produce steam and others incorporate a hair conditioner, excessive use can result in dry, heat-damaged hair.

Rollers/Curlers

Hair needs to be damp when using curlers so that it is easy to manage and will dry in a curled style. Hair can be left to dry naturally but using a hairdryer will speed up the process considerably. Using a setting lotion on the hair will help retain the curl for a longer time.

Hair Care Products

Shampoos

Shampoos are specially formulated for different hair types. There are also medicated shampoos, to treat dandruff, and shampoos for damaged or over-permed hair. Some shampoos are especially mild so that they can be used daily without having a harsh effect on the hair. Shampoos may also have special ingredients for specific purposes – egg for example is common as it is high in protein and conditions the hair. Avocado, herbs, henna and coconut or olive oil are frequently added to shampoos.

Conditioners

These are used after shampooing. Some shampoos actually contain a conditioner, although this is not as effective as using a separate conditioner. Conditioners help to add shine and body and make the hair easier to comb through. It is sufficient to use a conditioner once a week.

Deep conditioning treatments can help repair damaged hair. These should be used less frequently than ordinary conditioners and need to be left on the hair for a longer period to allow them to penetrate. It is a good idea to use one of these every two to three weeks on dry or normal hair.

Setting Lotions

These come in liquid form, mousses and gels. Whatever type is preferred they all do basically the same job – hold curl.

Hairsprays

Hairsprays hold a hairstyle in place. They should not be used too often as they tend to have a drying effect on the hair.

Colourants

Highlighting Shampoos

These add highlights to hair and wash out each time the hair is shampooed. They are cheap, easy to use and mild to hair.

Semi-permanent Colourants

These are applied to the hair after shampooing. Dark hair cannot be lightened but the colour change can be quite apparent. They last for between three and twelve weeks, when the colour just fades out.

Tints

These are permanent colourants which should preferably be applied by a professional hairdresser to be sure of a good result. Some people are allergic to the chemicals in tints so it is wise to have a patch test 48 hours before colouring the hair. It is necessary to have regular touch-ups of the roots as the hair grows out, about once a month. Tinted hair must be well-cared for using mild, non-medicated shampoos and conditioners as it is more easily damaged than non-tinted hair.

Bleaches

Bleaches make the hair blonde by bleaching out the hair's natural colour. The colour is permanent which means that roots have to be retouched continually. They tend to have a drying effect on the hair, making it more susceptible to damage.

Highlights

These are for streaking hair. They do not weaken hair or require retouching.

Henna Hair Colourant

Henna powder comes from the henna plant. There are two types – neutral henna and red henna. The first is a conditioner and does not colour the hair. Red henna, applied to the hair as a paste and left for several hours will colour the hair. The intensity of the colour will depend on the hair's natural colour and how long it is left on.

Perming the Hair

A perm can give body to the hair, gently wave it or provide a mass of curls. It is a chemical process applied in two stages. First perming lotion is applied and then a neutraliser. Well-permed hair can, for a period of months, until it grows out, be easier to style and manage. Perming solutions can have other effects on the hair, however, besides curling it. The chemicals can lighten the hair colour and dry it out. Permed hair is more vulnerable to damage and so should be cared for by conditioning it regularly and treating it gently. It is a good idea to condition the hair before a perm and most hairdressers advise not using a hair dryer for a few days afterwards.

How To Wash Hair

▶ Comb or brush the hair.
▶ Wet hair with *warm* water – hot water is not good for the hair.
▶ Pour a small amount of shampoo into palm of hand and apply to hair (make sure shampoo matches hair type).

▶ Massage shampoo into scalp for a few minutes.
▶ Rinse hair thoroughly. Shampoo left in the hair can cause dandruff and will dull the hair.
▶ If hair is particularly dirty, shampoo and rinse again in the same way, otherwise one application is sufficient.
▶ Gently squeeze out water from hair.
▶ (This next step is optional) Pour a small amount of conditioner into hand and rub hands together before applying to hair. Comb hair through (do this carefully as wet hair is vulnerable). Leave for time indicated (usually one minute).
▶ Rinse out thoroughly.
▶ Pat hair with a towel to remove water. Do not rub.
▶ Proceed with preferred styling method.

Hair should be washed at least once a week, and preferably twice, to keep it looking clean and shiny. Some people like to wash their hair every day. Mild shampoos are specially formulated for daily washing.

How to Use a Hairdresser/Barber

When making a first visit to a hairdressers it is a good idea to find one which is recommended by someone you know and whose hair has been well cut and styled. It is important anyway to give the stylist as good an idea as possible of what style you want. Take a picture along if you have one.

Try to make an appointment either by going in or phoning on a day or at a time when you know that the hairdresser will not be very busy so that the stylist can devote his or her time to you and not be in a hurry. A Monday is good; Saturday is the worst day. Not all hairdressers require an appointment to be made.

It is not essential to tip a hairdresser or barber but if you are pleased with the job they have done and would like to show your appreciation by giving a tip, a rule of thumb is to give about 10% of the cost.

Some women's hairdressers cater for young women, have all the latest equipment and style hair in the latest fashion. Others are more obviously for the older woman and do more traditional styles. Some hairdressers are unisex and cater for both men and women, often washing, cutting and styling hair in the same general areas.

How often one should go to a hairdresser or barber depends on several factors. Hair grows on average about ½" a month, although some people's hair grows faster than others. To keep short hair looking tidy and well groomed it usually needs to be cut once every 6 to 9 weeks. Long hair does not necessarily require cutting as frequently. Many women like to have their hair shampooed and set once a week. Frequency of visits also depends to some extent on the condition of the hair.

The cost of a visit depends on the service required. A cut and blow-dry, the most frequent service for women, will be a lot cheaper than a perm. Hairdressers prices vary tremendously so it is worth shopping around. Many of them have hairdressing students; those that do will often provide a free hairdo or charge a very nominal fee if you allow a student to do your hair. The students are very carefully supervised so it is unlikely they will make any serious mistakes. Students are usually taught outside the shop's normal hours so the appointment will probably be for an evening rather than during the day.

Hair Care for Black People

The hair of black men and women is often dry and brittle. Over-use of hair-dryers and other appliances can further damage the hair and aggravate the problem. It is a good idea therefore to apply an oil treatment every so often: massage warm oil into the hair and cover with a plastic shower cap for about 30 minutes. Then shampoo hair thoroughly, removing all traces of oil.

Styling Techniques

Relaxing
The natural kink in the hair is temporarily removed and the hair straightened, making a wider range of hair styles possible.

Extensions
New hair is woven into existing hair. Extensions can be added to create plaits all around the head. Beads or ribbons can be included for decoration.

Perming
Hair is straightened, using a special cream, then wound on to large rollers. A neutralising solution is then applied and the hair conditioned after the rollers have been removed.

Head Lice

Infestation with head lice is relatively common and does not reflect on the cleanliness of the head. Head lice are passed on rapidly by head contact so people living and working in close proximity to each other are vulnerable. The louse which is the size of a pin head and thus difficult to see, lays up to 300 white eggs, called nits, which become firmly attached to the hairs. They feed on blood and the bites cause severe itching, commonly at the nape of the neck or behind the ears.

What to Look For

Run a fine-toothed comb through parted hair and look carefully for traces on the comb.

Sometimes tiny inflamed bites on the scalp are visible.

Treatment

1) Special lotions and shampoos for treating head lice are available from all chemists (eg. Prioderm and Carylderm). It is important to follow the instructions on the packaging.

2) Inform people with whom you are in close contact that you have head lice. However it is important that all the people who live with you are treated at the same time to prevent the lice from passing back and forth thus causing reinfection and the continuity of the problem.

3) Don't be embarrassed: having head lice is no longer a social stigma, as they thrive on clean heads.

Discussion Topics

● Special hair problems and effective ways of dealing with them.
● How content are members with the condition and style of their hair?
● What current regimes do individual group members follow in caring for their hair?

Practical Activities

▶ Place on a table as many different types of equipment as possible. For example, shampoos and conditioners, heated rollers, curling tongs, hair slides and combs, hair dryers, heated brushes, home perms, etc. Demonstrate how they are used and invite members to try them out.

▶ If available, a women's hairdresser or a barber can be invited to attend a group and teach styling techniques or use of equipment.

Recipes

Setting Lotions

Cheap but effective alternatives to commercial setting lotions are beer or lemon juice. Beer gives body and lemon juice is especially good for fair or greasy hair. Sugar water can also be used. One teaspoon of sugar should be dissolved in a cup of boiling water; use it when it is cool. Each of these is easier to use if put into a spray bottle.

Hair lightener for light brown or fair hair

This recipe creates highlights in hair when exposed to the sun. Make up a rinse using one part lemon juice to four parts water. Pour on partly dried hair, and let it dry naturally.

11: SKIN CARE

Protecting the Skin

The skin's needs change with age. When we are young the natural moisture of the skin keeps it smooth and supple. As we grow older it loses some of its firmness and wrinkles appear. The harsh effects of the weather and the drying effect of central heating can accelerate these changes. However, keeping the skin clean and protected can help to some extent. Washing the face, using warm water and mild soap is basically all that is needed. Commercial products available can provide extra care. These are often designed for specific types of skin – usually normal, dry, oily, combination and/or sensitive.

General Rules for Healthy Skin

▶ Eat a healthy balanced diet. Fresh fruit and vegetables are good for the skin. Sweet things and spicy, fried or starchy foods can cause spots or oily skin.

▶ Fresh air and exercise help to stimulate the skin and improve the blood supply.

▶ Do not touch spots – let the skin renew itself in its own time to prevent scarring or blemishes.

▶ Wash the face night and morning to keep the skin clean.

▶ Make sure that flannels and towels are clean to prevent skin infections occurring.

▶ Acne is a skin problem common to young adults, for which help may be necessary. Regular hygiene, a regular diet with plenty of fibre to avoid constipation, enough sleep and clean towels and flannels will also help. Interfering with spots is likely to spread the infection.

▶ Dandruff can cause spots on the face, so a dandruff treatment shampoo should be used if necessary.

▶ If a facial product is causing redness of the skin or a rash it should be discarded and another product used instead, possibly a purer type which is less likely to irritate the skin.

For Women:

Make-up

Make-up is not necessary for an attractive and well-groomed appearance. Some women however like to wear it every day and would not feel properly "dressed" without it. Others wear make-up only for social occasions. It is not necessary to use the whole range of cosmetics when making-up. Just making up the eyes for example, or the lips, or the skin, without applying make-up to other areas of the face can be perfectly satisfactory if it is done well.

Products are often available in different forms. For example, a blusher can be bought as a pressed powder, gel, pencil or as a cream. These all do essentially the same job. Following these guidelines will help when applying make-up.

Foundations

A foundation is not necessary with a clear, glowing skin that has a good colour. To hide blemishes and provide a little colour to a pale skin a foundation can be used. It also provides a good "canvas" to work on. For young skin a light cream or liquid foundation should be used. Foundations come in different shades and should be chosen to match as closely as possible the colour of the skin. Testers are often available to try out before making a purchase. The choice however should not depend on colour alone but also on age and type of skin.

Application

A moisturiser should always be used on the skin before applying foundation as it will then go on more evenly. It also prevents the foundation from entering and blocking the skin's pores. Apply small dots of foundation to the forehead, chin, nose and cheeks. Blend it in with the fingertips, always in an upward direction. It should be blended over the jaw bone and on down the throat to avoid leaving a line. If too much has been applied the excess should be removed with cotton wool or a tissue.

Blushers

Blusher is used to emphasise the line of the cheekbones and to add colour to the cheeks. The shade chosen should work with the complexion. Powder blusher is easier to apply. It is applied with a large, fluffy make-up brush (but a cotton wool ball will also do the job satisfactorily) and swept lightly along the cheekbones from the top of the cheeks at the hairline, to the centre of the cheeks.

Eye Colour

There are many eye products on the market of every conceivable shade and new ones are being created all the time, so there should be eye make-up to suit everybody. The important thing is not to overdo it, and to avoid hard lines. Make-up should enhance the eyes and make them look more attractive. There are no hard and fast rules about colours. Shadows do not have to match eye colour or clothes. Neutral colours are easier for the inexperienced to apply than deeper colours. Eye shadow should follow the lines and contours of the eye. For basic shading, the following guidelines may be useful:

▶ In the socket area use a mid-tone shadow blending outwards to the outer corner of the eye. The darker the tone the deeper set the eye becomes.

▶ A dark tone should then be used at the base of the top and bottom lashes to enhance the shape of the eye.

▶ A light tone can be used to shade the inner corner of the eye or middle of the lid to highlight.

Eyeliner

This is optional. Liquid liners create a hard line. Cake liners need to be mixed with water and are softer. It is easier to make a light shade with these. A good eyeliner brush should be used to paint a line from one side of the eye to the other, close to the base of the top lashes.

Alternatively the line could begin at mid-eye. Painting the lower lid in the same way is a matter of personal choice if it suits the person wearing it. Powder shadow lightly brushed over liner can soften it further.

Eyebrows

Eyebrows can simply be brushed into shape using a dry toothbrush. Plucking the brows can be difficult and painful and the hard line that is often the result of plucking does not look very natural. However, very heavy brows can be thinned out by using a pair of eyebrow tweezers. Only one hair at a time should be plucked, always from beneath the brow, never from the top and in a quick firm movement. Pale eyebrows can benefit from using an eyebrow pencil for definition.

Lashes

Mascara is the finishing touch to eyes. The waterproof type is advisable as it avoids smudging. Mascara can darken, colour, thicken and lengthen lashes. Applying it may take practice to prevent lashes clogging together. The top lashes can be brushed above and below from the base to the tip, or just from below. The bottom lashes are brushed from above. Any smudges on the skin can be removed with a cotton bud dipped in eye make-up remover.

Lip Colour

For long-lasting, non-smear lip colour, lipstick should be applied this way:

▶ Apply foundation to lips and dust lightly with powder.

▶ Outline the lips with a brush or sharpened lip pencil. The colour chosen should tone with lip colour. The natural line of the mouth can be changed, for example, the lower lip made fuller, by careful corrective outlining.

▶ Fill in with matching lipstick. Blot with a tissue then repeat this last step. A dab of lip gloss in the centre of the lower lip can be effective.

Equipment

This is the equipment needed for applying make-up. The items may not all be necessary depending on what make-up is used. All equipment will last longer and be more effective if kept properly clean:

Mirror
Set of brushes for eyes, lips, blushers and powder
Cosmetic sponges
Cotton buds
Tissues
Pencil sharpener
Towelling band or scarf
Tweezers
Cotton wool
Sponge applicators
Powder-puff

Make-up Tips

▶ Always make up in a good light.
▶ Make-up for evening should be stronger.
▶ Pin back hair when making up so that the face is easier to work on and make-up does not get in hair.
▶ Don't pluck eyebrows just before making up.
▶ Remove all traces of make-up before bedtime to keep skin clean and prevent pores becoming blocked which could cause blackheads.

Economies

▶ A soft toilet roll can be substituted for tissues.
▶ Use cotton wool which comes in a roll. It is made in layers. Unroll it and then cut 2-inch or 3-inch squares. Peel off the layers. You then have lots of cotton wool pads for removing make-up.
▶ The little bit of lipstick usually left in the container and thrown away can be used for outlining. A lip brush can easily reach in.

Face Packs or Masks

For toning, tightening and refreshing the skin. Masks are available for all types of skin and can be applied once or twice a week. A good idea is to combine a relaxation session with applying a face-mask. Apply the mask and, resting on something comfortable, lay down on the floor with feet raised up; close the eyes and relax for fifteen minutes to half an hour before washing the mask off. Masks made up of raw materials are often as effective and certainly cheaper than commercial ones.

Hair Removal

Removal of body hair is a matter of personal choice and is an aspect of grooming that changes with fashion. There are several different methods some of which are for specific areas of the body. The choice of hair removal products will depend to some extent on how extensive or coarse the hair is, hair colour, cost, convenience and skin sensitivity. It is a good idea after removing hair to moisturise the skin with a perfume free moisturiser. Most chemical-based hair removers and bleaching creams recommend doing a patch test to ensure that there is no allergic reaction, before using the product. After removing underarm hair, skin will be more sensitive than usual and it is wise not to use a deodorant for at least 24 hours. For this reason it's a good idea to remove underarm hair at night before going to bed.

For Men:

Shaving

Shaving becomes necessary at different ages for men. Some men of course choose to grow beards or moustaches and no longer need a full shave. Hygiene and regular trimming then become important to maintain a good appearance.

How to Shave Using a Safety Razor

▶ The face should be washed with soap and warm water before shaving. This will soften the bristles and reduce the risk of dirt entering open pores and causing infection. Leave the skin wet.
▶ Apply lather. This also helps soften the bristles and enables the razor blade to move easily across the surface of the skin.

▶ Shave the softest parts of the beard first and the hardest parts last. The latter will be the most resistant to shaving. Use downward strokes to begin with. Many men find it easier to shave in this order: sides, neck and under chin, chin, moustache. Then use the razor from various directions ending with upward strokes to smooth off.

▶ Rinse away all traces of soap with warm water.

▶ Rinse razor with very hot water.

▶ Splash either cold water or after shave on to the skin to close the pores. Water does an adequate job but in addition to closing the pores, after-shave adds fragrance and sterilises the skin. It has a tendency however to have a drying effect on the skin.

Using an Electric Razor

The biggest benefit of an electric razor is convenience. Shaving cream and water are unnecessary although many men still splash on cold water or aftershave afterwards to tighten the skin and close pores. The disadvantages are the cost of buying one and the fact that a safety razor will give a closer shave.

Shaving Tips

▶ Most men find it necessary to shave every morning. If going out in the evening, another shave is usually required to maintain a well-groomed appearance.

▶ Most men use aerosol foams or creams these days; some however still prefer to use shaving soap and a brush. It is important to rinse the brush thoroughly after use or it will become dirty and harbour bacteria. Keeping it clean will also preserve its bushiness.

▶ Electric razors should be cleaned regularly to maintain their performance.

▶ It is necessary to replace the blades in both a safety razor and an electric razor when they start doing a less than adequate job, otherwise there will be an increased risk of nicking the skin.

▶ To avoid infection spreading, ensure that *all* trimming and shaving equipment is kept clean.

▶ Do not share razors.

▶ A styptic pencil will staunch the flow of blood when applied to a cut incurred while shaving.

DISCUSSION TOPICS:

(Women or Men)
● What is each member's daily cleansing routine?
● Do any members have any particular skin problems, eg spots, dryness, sensitivity, etc?
● What methods are used to deal with problem areas?

(Women)
● What is each member's make-up routine?
● Has it changed at all in the last few years?
● Is there any type of make-up members would like to practise with that they haven't tried before?
● Make a group collage using magazine pictures to demonstrate 'Rules for Healthy Skin.'

(Men)
● How often does each member shave?
● How often do they change their blades?
● Do they adopt a particular method when shaving or is it a haphazard affair?
● What products do they use, for example do they use after-shave?

Make-up

▶ Each person is asked to bring to a group session their make-up bag. These are displayed and discussed. Members are invited to talk about how they use particular items.

▶ Apply make-up to one half of a person's face, teaching them each step. Then they make up the other half using the same techniques.

▶ Invite a beautician (from the Red Cross perhaps) or else a person who is particularly skilled and knowledgeable about skin care and make-up to demonstrate the use of cosmetics.

▶ Draw a face on each of several pieces of blotting-paper and give one to each group member to try out samples of make-up by dabbing them on the face.

▶ Use a large diagram of a face indicating where to apply make-up and which colours to use.

▶ Make up some of the following recipes and try them out.

Recipes

Home-made face masks

Egg white mask (for oily skin)
Beat an egg white until frothy. Spread thinly over face until set. Rinse off with warm water.

Lemon mask (for oily skin)
Mix together milk, lemon juice and oatmeal to a thick paste. Spread on face. Leave for ten minutes and rinse off with cold water.

Egg white mask (for dry skin)
Same as for oily skin except add one teaspoon of oil.

Banana mask (for dry skin)
Mash up a banana and add to it a small amount of warmed oil. Apply to face, leave on for fifteen minutes, then rinse.

Milk and juice masks
Dampen a piece of cotton wool with milk and apply it to the face. Wash off after 15 minutes. Try using fruit juice.

Home-made Cleansers

Potato cleanser
Cut a potato in half and rub it over the face.

Rosewater wash
An ordinary soap and water wash can be perfumed with rosewater or an essential oil, such as sandalwood.

Old-fashioned steam clean
The skin can be steamed, for 10 to 15 minutes about once a week to open blocked pores, remove blackheads, and improve circulation. Pour boiling water into a bowl. Put your face over the steam – but no nearer than about 30cm (approx 1 foot) – and cover the head with a towel to prevent the steam escaping. Rosewater, lavender or a herb such as rosemary can be added to the water. Blackheads can be removed using cotton wool. Then use a skin tonic to close the pores and tighten the skin.

Home-made Toners

Lemon Toner (oily skin)
Squeeze the juice of half a lemon into one cup of water. Dampen cotton wool with solution and wipe gently to remove surface oil.

Rosewater Tonic
Dampen cotton wool in rosewater and wipe over face.

Rosewater and Witch-hazel Tonic (oily skin)
Stir these together in equal quantities and apply.

Vinegar Tonic
One part vinegar to eight parts water. Stir. Use for washing.

Shaving

▶ A volunteer from the group is asked to demonstrate his shaving method using a safety razor. The member then proceeds to shave saying what he is doing and why at each stage. Other members are free to make comments. Alternatively, this can be done on an individual basis.

▶ Each member is asked to bring to a group session their shaving equipment. The equipment is displayed and discussed. Members are invited to talk about how they use particular items.

▶ Shave one half of a member's face teaching them each step. Then they shave the other half using the same techniques.

OBJECTIVES:

● To increase awareness of the need for regular hygiene.
● To improve the appearance of hands and nails.

Care of the Skin

Hands are instantly noticeable, need to be well-cared for and kept clean. They need to be washed after each visit to the toilet and before preparation of food as they are constantly in contact with germs. Frequent contact with water, however, especially hard water, can cause dry, rough or chapped skin. Detergents and commonly used household cleansers also have a drying effect. Here are some guidelines for hand care.

Care of Hands and Nails

▶ Keep hands clean by washing regularly with soap and water.

▶ Use a nail brush to keep nails clean. Underneath the nails is where many micro-organisms collect.

▶ Rubber gloves will protect hands when doing washing up or dirty household jobs.

▶ Wearing warm gloves in cold weather will prevent redness and dry skin.

▶ Keep nails trimmed. They are easier to take care of if kept short. This can be done with either nail scissors or an emery board. A nail file is not advisable as it leaves a ragged edge.

▶ Stains on nails caused by nicotine can be removed by cleaning with a nail brush dipped in fresh lemon juice.

▶ Nail biting causes weak nails and also takes dirt into the mouth quite apart from making nails unattractive.

▶ Use hand cream for sore or dry skin. If necessary medicated hand cream can be obtained from the chemist.

A Ten-Minute Manicure

Step 1
Wash hands and clean nails with a nail brush. Dry thoroughly with a towel.

Step 2
Shape nails into rounded edges with the fine side of an emery board. Move board from side to centre in one movement. Moving board back and forth creates ragged edges. Do not file too low at sides.

Step 3
Soak fingers in warm soapy water for 5 minutes.

Step 4
Dry hands then gently push back cuticles with an orange stick covered at the tip by cotton wool; or use a cotton bud. Cuticle cream can be used for this job but it is not essential.

Step 5
Rub hand cream into hands to prevent dryness. After drying hands, cuticles can be pushed back with the towel. Do not cut cuticles with scissors.

For Women:

Applying Nail Polish

Clean, well cared for nails make hands look attractive in both men and women. Some women like to use nail polish after a manicure.

Apply polish ideally at bedtime. It will then dry hard overnight. It should only be used on well-shaped unbitten nails. Before applying nail polish all traces of grease should be removed by washing nails with soapy water and a nailbrush, otherwise polish will not adhere.

Colour should be applied in three thin coats. This way it will last longer and give a better finish. It is important to let each coat dry thoroughly before applying the next. Each nail should be painted in three strokes, starting at the cuticle and moving brush along to nail tip. Paint the middle stroke first, then one either side.

Any smudges on fingers can be removed with cotton wool or cotton bud dipped in remover. Leave to harden for at least half an hour.

Nail polish should always be removed when it starts chipping off, and then reapplied.

Hand Care Kit

Suggested items for hand and nail care. These are not all essential items:

Hand cream
Nail brush
Orange stick
Emery board
Nail scissors
Nail polish remover
Cotton wool
Cotton buds
Nail strengthener
Cuticle cream
Nail polish

DISCUSSION TOPICS:

● What do our hands reflect about us?
● How do members take care of their hands, if at all?

Hand Drawing

Each person is asked to draw an outline round one of their hands on a piece of paper. This is repeated with the other hand so that they end up with a picture of two hands side by side. Each person then writes on the first hand all the things about their hands they are dissatisfied with. At the conclusion of the teaching session on hand care, they are then asked to write on the other hand remedies for improving their hands. So the end picture might look something like this:

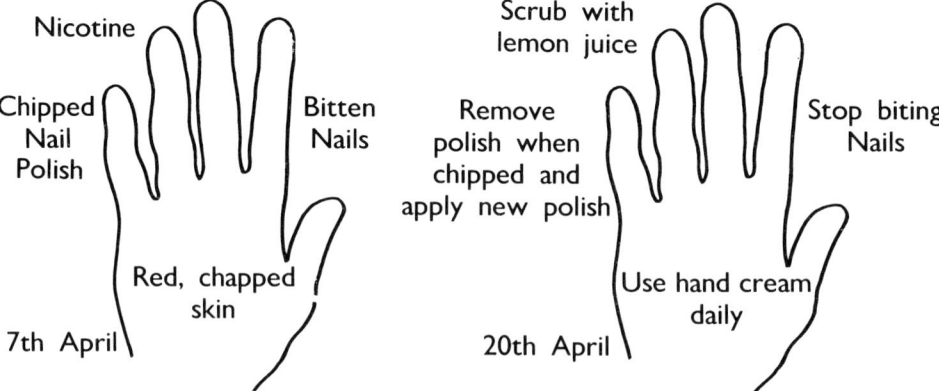

Nicotine
Chipped Nail Polish
Bitten Nails
Red, chapped skin
7th April

Scrub with lemon juice
Remove polish when chipped and apply new polish
Stop biting Nails
Use hand cream daily
20th April

▶ Try out manicures, cleansing techniques, etc in a practical group session.

Hand Milk Recipe

Ingredients: ½ cup milk
1 slice lemon

Method: Steep lemon in milk for approximately 3 hours or until milk has begun to curdle. Remove lemon and rub milk into hands to feed and soften skin. Keep hand milk in refrigerator.

SECTION 3

USEFUL ADDRESSES

The information provided below was correct at the time this manual was researched.

When requesting information from an organisation it is advisable to ascertain whether a publication is still available, its current cost, if any, and whether a self-addressed envelope is required.

"Recommended" indicates that publications have been personally reviewed and are recommended by the author.

Diet

▶ The British Nutrition Foundation

15 Belgrave Square
London SW1X 8PS
Tel: 071 235 4904

The role of this organisation is to provide information to promote education and to encourage research in food and nutrition. As part of this programme the Foundation prepares a wide variety of publications including books and leaflets on topical issues relating to food, nutrition and health.

Films and posters are available. For example (film): *A Way of Life* is about obesity and the value of prevention. 16mm colour, 24 mins. Films can be purchased or borrowed free.

▶ The British Heart Foundation

102 Gloucester Place
London W1H 4DH
Tel: 071 935 0185

Provides information leaflets. Regional Organisers (see British Heart Foundation in local telephone directories) can usually arrange speakers to talk about the work of the Foundation.

Recommended leaflets: *Reducing the Risk of a Heart Attack*; *Smoking and Your Heart*; *Is It Blood Pressure?*; *Diet and Your Heart*.

▶ The Ministry of Agriculture, Fisheries & Food

Great Westminster House
Horseferry Road
London SW1P 2AE
Tel: 071 216 6311

The Ministry's Food Science Division publishes books and booklets such as *The Manual of Nutrition* and *Look at the Label*.

▶ The National Dairy Council

National Dairy Centre
John Princes Street
London W1M 0AP
Tel: 071 499 7822

Publishes free booklets on health and nutrition. Recommended: *Take a Closer Look at Health*; *Take Something Simple* (recipes for men and women at retirement age); *Keeping Fit in Retirement* (advice for the retired on shopping, cooking and eating and other information); *Milk for Goodness Sake*; *Serves 1*.

▶ The Milk Marketing Board

Thames Ditton
Surrey
KT7 0EL
Tel: 081 398 4101

Runs a lecture service for groups of a minimum of 20 people, fee £20.00.

▶ The Flour Advisory Bureau Limited

21 Arlington Street
London SW1A 1RN
Tel: 071 493 2521

The Bureau operates a nutrition and cookery advisory service and an editorial recipe service. Sound nutrition and practical cookery are major themes of its work. It is designed to promote the use of flour and bread and provides literature and a consumer advice service.

Recommended leaflets: *Choosing Food for Health* (food guide for a healthy lifestyle); *Bread for Healthy Living* (recipes and keep-fit plan); *Sensible Slimming Wallchart*; *Choosing Food for Health*.

▶ The Kraft Kitchen Advisory Service

Kraft Food Limited
St Georges House
Bayshill Road, Cheltenham
Glos GL50 3AE
Tel: 0242 236101

Offers advice on a healthy diet and cookery problems. Recommended leaflets: *No Waste Cookery*; *Healthy Living Recipes* (includes a metric conversion chart and seasonal foods chart. Recipes have symbols to indicate information such as amount of fibre or fat).

▶ **The Potato Marketing Board**
50 Hans Crescent
Knightsbridge, London SW1X 0NB
Tel: 071 589 4874

Provides information to the general public and health professionals on the subject of potatoes. Speakers and demonstrators available throughout the country. The Board's Cookery Demonstration Service is intended to show interesting ways of serving potatoes, using recipes taken from the current cookery leaflets and which emphasise the versatility of the potato in the household menu. Copies of the leaflets are distributed at the meeting. The demonstration lasts approximately one hour and includes a short quiz for which prizes are awarded. As well as the free recipe leaflets, a Potato Cookery Book is available for purchase at a special price.

Recommended leaflets: *Down to Earth with British Potatoes*; *Potato Pete's Special Recipes*; *Nutritional Value of Potatoes*. Posters: *Potato Pete's Guide to Great British Potatoes*; *Potato Pete's Guide to New Potatoes*.

▶ **The Coeliac Society**
PO Box 220
High Wycombe
Bucks
HP11 2HY

Offers information on diet to people suffering from coeliac condition. For example the Society produces a booklet listing special foods which are sold in ordinary shops and are gluten-free. A colour film and a tape recorded lecture are available on loan.

Fitness

▶ **The Sports Council**
16 Upper Woburn Place
London WC1H 0QP
Tel: 071 388 1277

The Information Centre contains an extensive reference collection of literature (books and magazines) on all aspects of sport and physical recreation, including publications on exercise and fitness. The Centre is open for use by the public Monday to Friday, 9am to 5pm. It is not necessary to make an appointment.

Recommended publications: *The Case for Exercise – Research Paper*; *Keep in Touch . . . With Sports Council Publications*; *50+ Take Time to Play Safely* (medical advice on activity for older people); *50+ All to Play For: Sport in the Community – The Next Ten Years*.

▶ **The Scottish Sports Council**
Caledonia House,
South Gyle,
Edinburgh EH12 9DQ.
Tel: 031 317 7200

The Council provides an advisory service on physical fitness. They also work in conjunction with the Scottish Sports Association and the Consultative Group on Sports Medicine and Sports Sciences. They promote research into aspects of fitness, such as fitness testing and have run campaigns to encourage improved fitness through sport. They provide an advisory service and make available speakers, leaflets, guides and general advisory documents.

▶ **The Sports Council for Northern Ireland**
House of Sport
Upper Malone Road
Belfast BT9 5LA
Tel: 0232 381222

Speakers available using A/V equipment. Advisory leaflets, for example: *Fun Runs: Guidelines for Organisers*. Information booklets, for example: *Jogging and Running Clubs*. Promotion leaflets, for example: *Cycling, swimming, yoga*, etc. Reports, ie, *Reflections on Stress*. Newsletters.

▶ **St Andrew's Ambulance Association**
St Andrew's House
48 Milton Street
Glasgow G4 OHR
Tel: 041 332 4031

Voluntary organisation whose primary aim is instruction and training in First Aid; regularly runs courses in First Aid.

Women's Health Care

▶ **Smith & Nephew Consumer Products Ltd**
Alum Rock Road
Birmingham B8 3DZ
Tel: 021 327 4750

Produces educational material on women's health matters. Recommended leaflets: *The Lilia-White Advisory Service – The Menopause, what it is and how to cope*; *The Lilia-White Advisory Service – Premenstrual Tension, what is it?*; *Body Talk*; *Growing Up*; *Lil-lets leaflet* (Informative and detailed explanation on internal sanitary protection); *Female Reproductive Organs leaflet* (Diagrams of the reproductive organs one side with the menstrual cycle illustrated on the reverse).

Recommended Wall Chart: Large clear diagram of the female reproductive organs.

▶ **Women's National Cancer Control Campaign**
1 South Audley Street
London W1Y 5DQ
Tel: 071 499 7532

They aim to promote preventive care with regard to cervical cancer and breast cancer.

Recommended leaflets: *Calling All Women* (information on the smear test); *Your Life in Your Hands* (information on breast self-examination).

Birth Control & Sexual Health

▶ **The Family Planning Association**
27/35 Mortimer Street
London W1N 7RJ
Tel: 071 636 7866 (Information)
       071 631 0555 (Administration)

The Family Planning Association is a charity which monitors and comments on family planning and related services in Britain. The two main threads of its work are information (through the Family Planning Information Service) and education. The FPA's Education Unit runs courses for professionals on all aspects of personal and sexual relationships. The Unit also provides resources for those involved in sex education. At the FPA's national office there is also a Book Centre and book mail order department. A wide range of books is available; topics include: contraception, sexuality, sex education, pregnancy, abortion, child and family health, subfertility, STDs and population issues.

The Family Planning Information Service (run jointly by the FPA and the Health Education Authority) offers a free phone-in and write-in advice and information service on all aspects of contraception, sexuality and personal relationships. The Central Enquiries Department (071 636 7866) also keeps details of all family planning clinics, help agencies and related services. Free leaflets and posters are available from FPIS on contraception methods and services (sae appreciated). Professionals may use the Resource Centre for research.

Recommended leaflets: *Basic Information on Family Planning for Nurses, Pharmacists, Social Workers and All Who May Be Asked for Advice*; *Basics of Birth Control*; *Pills in Perspective, a Consumer Guide for Women Who Take Oral Contraceptives*; *The Pill*; *Barrier Methods of Birth Control*; *Intrauterine Devices*; *The Family Planning Information Service Order Form*; *All About Family Planning Services*.

Dental Care

▶ **British Dental Health Foundation**
Eastlands Court
St Peter's Road
Rugby
Warwickshire
CV21 3QP

The Foundation is a registered charity whose aim is to improve public dental health by education and public relations means. To do this it produces a fairly comprehensive range of materials. It assists the general public by answering enquiries on dental matters, or sending free of charge, leaflets, if requests are accompanied by a stamped self-addressed envelope.

Recommended leaflets: *Tell Me About Eating Well and Staying Biting Fit*; *Tell Me About Orthodontics*; *Tell Me About Partial Dentures and Bridges*; *Tell Me About Crowns*; *Tell Me About Preventive Dentistry and Oral Hygiene*; *Selecting a Dentist*.

▶ **Stafford-Miller Ltd**
45 Broadwater Road
Welwyn Garden City
Herts AL7 3SP
Tel: 0707 331001

This company provides assistance to the general public and health professionals. It offers a comprehensive range of patient education literature on all aspects of dental care direct to all consumers who express an interest.

Recommended leaflets: *Stafford-Miller Dental Care Products*; *About Your Dentures*.

Eye Care

▶ **Optical Information Council**
Temple Chambers
Temple Avenue
London EC4 0DT
Tel: 071 353 3556

Provides information on matters relating to the function and care of sight.

Recommended leaflets: *Care for Your Sight*; *So You're Partially Sighted*; *Beginning with Bifocals*; *What You Need to Know About Sunglasses*.

▶ **The Association of Contact Lens Manufacturers Ltd**
PO Box 12
Bishops Waltham
Southampton
SO3 12I
Tel: 0489 895791

The ACLM provides information to the public on contact lenses, solutions and ancillary products, their availability and use.

The Association also answers individual queries from members of the public through the Public Relations Executive:
Mrs Elizabeth Smith
Chartham
Branksome Park Road
Camberley
Surrey GU15 2AQ
Tel: 0276 28964

Recommended leaflets: *Contact Lenses – Your Questions Answered*; *You Can See the Difference*.

Foot Care

▶ **The Society of Chiropodists**
53 Welbeck Street
London W1M 7HE
Tel: 071 486 3381/4

Provides leaflets, booklets, posters. Recommended leaflets: *Care of Your Feet*; *Feet Grown Old*; *Care of the Feet for Diabetics*.

▶ **Newtons Laboratories**
111-113 Wandsworth High Street
London SW18 4HY
Tel: 081 874 6511

Offers printed information on their footcare products. Recommended leaflet: *Do You Suffer with Foot Problems?*

▶ **Cuxson, Gerrard and Co (Dressings) Ltd**
26 Fountain Lane
Oldbury, Warley
West Midlands B69 3BB
Tel: 021 552 1355

A company manufacturing a wide range of products including footcare items. They produce a guide (recommended) to aid people in caring for and treating painful conditions of their feet, called *Spring Into Step*. The leaflet is free to the general public on receipt of a self addressed stamped envelope.

Clothes

▶ **British Apparel Centre**
7 Swallow Place
London W1R 7AA
Tel: 071 408 0020

A voluntary organisation concerned with the laundering and dry-cleaning of clothes and textiles offering leaflets to the general public.
Recommended leaflets: *The International Textile Care Labelling Code – What It Means to You*; *Care Labelling Symbols Guide – Conditions of Use*.

▶ **Textiles Services Association**
7 Churchill Court
58 Station Rd
North Harrow
Middlesex HA2 7SA
Tel: 081 863 9177

A Trade Association mainly serving its members. However, there is a department within the Association, The Drycleaning Information Bureau (DIB), which has been set up to answer queries from the general public, which may vary from how to remove various types of stains to where one can get an ostrich feathered hat cleaned. The DIB has a separate telephone number: 081 863 8658.

There are two leaflets available to the general public upon request: *What Your Drycleaner Can Do For You* (an information leaflet for drycleaning customers) and *Fabric and Garment Care* (helpful hints on buying and cleaning fabrics and clothes) (Recommended).

Hair Care

▶ **The Institute of Trichologists**
228 Stockwell Road
Brixton, London SW9 9SU
Tel: 071 733 2056

Offers to the public leaflets on haircare and arranges for speakers, etc where possible. Will, upon receipt of a stamped self-addressed envelope, supply the names and addresses of local practitioners to enquirers.
Recommended leaflet: *Your Hair and Its Care*.

▶ **Napp Laboratories**
The Science Park
Cambridge CB4 4GW
Tel: 0223 424444

Produces an information leaflet on head lice.

Skin Care

▶ **Almay**
225 Bath Road
Slough SL1 4AU
Tel: 0753 23971

Provides leaflets to the general public and assistance to those who suffer from allergies or sensitivity to cosmetics. Recommended leaflets: *Every Woman's Guide to Skin Care*; *Making Eyes*; *Making Faces*.

General

Under this title are listed organisations which provide informational material on more than one topic.

▶ **Health Education Authority**
Hamilton House
Mabledon Place
London WC1H 9TX
Tel: 071 383 3833
(Serving England, Northern Ireland and Wales)

▶ **The Scottish Health Education Group**
Woodburn House
Canaan Lane
Edinburgh EH10 4SG
(Serving Scotland)

Publications: Numerous leaflets and posters on health-related topics, with the emphasis on preventing ill health. These are obtainable in the first instance via local health education units which are part of each District Health Authority or equivalent. The address and phone number can be obtained from the library. (Some Units are known as Health "Promotion" Units). A free publications catalogue is available. There is also a quarterly journal available on subscription *(Health Education Journal)*; and a free newspaper *(Health Education News)* issued six times a year.

Resources Centre: The Council has a Resources Centre, consisting of a lending library, a reference only multi-media collection and an information service. This is open to the public Monday to Friday, 9am to 5pm. It is closed on public holidays and at weekends, and opens at 10am on the first Thursday of each month. A leaflet is issued outlining the services available, and listing the "source list" series of materiographies originating with the centre. There is also a free film catalogue. The Council is also an information provider on Prestel, lead frame 544.

Recommended leaflets and booklets: *Take a Look at Yourself*; *Foot Health* (Publications and Teaching Aids Source List); *Food for Thought*; *The Change of Life*; *Looking After Yourself*; *Cystitis*; *The Traffic Light Guide to Staying Slim*; *Fibre in Your Food*.

▶ **CFL Vision**
PO Box 35
Wetherby
West Yorkshire LS23 7EX
Tel: 0937 541010

Distributes educational, training and general information, films and videos of interest to the general public and/or health professionals. They provide a catalogue along with a copy of the Health Education Authority's catalogue as they distribute their programmes. Some titles are available on free loan, others on low-cost hire, and some are available for purchase.

▶ **Disabled Living Foundation**
380-384 Harrow Road
London W9 2HU
Tel: 071 289 6111

This organisation is a charitable trust, the terms of reference of which include all disabilities, mental, physical and sensory, together with multiple handicaps and the infirmities of age. The DLF is concerned with those aspects of ordinary life which present particular problems to disabled people of any age. The information available is provided to the general public and to health professionals although the latter need to be employed by a subscribing authority. Services offered include an Aids Demonstration Centre, leaflets on equipment and an enquiry service. Courses and seminars are arranged and speakers may sometimes be provided.

Recommended leaflets: *Clothing*; *Incontinence*; *Visual Handicap*.

▶ **Aids**

For information about AIDS, use these numbers:

Health Information Trust (Healthline) 081 980 6263

Terrence Higgins Trust 071 831 0330 or 071 242 1010 (helpline open 3–10 pm daily)

Scottish Aids Monitor 0345 090966

London Lesbian and Gay Switchboard 071 837 7324